Saint Joan of Arc

Virgin-Soldier

by Leon Cristiani

Translated from the French by
M. Angeline Bouchard

Pauline

ST. PAUL BOOKS & MEDIA

Imprimatur: ✠Humberto Cardinal Medeiros
Archbishop of Boston

Original French title: *Sainte Jeanne d' Arc*

Nihil Obstat: Jean Gautier, PSS

Imprimatur: Michel Potevin, v.g.

Cover Art: Giraudon/Art Resource, NY PFC 4619.
Jean-Jaques Scherrer (19th c. French): Joan of Arc
leaving 23 February 1429. Vaucouleurs, Hotel de
Ville.

Library of Congress Catalog Card Number: 74-16747

ISBN 0-8198-0466-5

Printed and published in the U.S.A. by St. Paul Books & Media,
50 St. Paul's Avenue, Boston, MA 02130.

St. Paul Books & Media is the publishing house of the Daughters of
St. Paul, an international congregation of women religious serving the
Church with the communications media.

5 6 7 8 9   99 98 97 96 95 94

Contents

1

Childhood in Domremy

A FLOWER OF FRENCH HISTORY

It is with joy and trembling that I begin this work. With joy, because there are few such beautiful and noble subjects. With trembling, too, because so much has already been written about Joan of Arc! Few historical figures have held greater attraction for writers of every nuance, both believers and unbelievers. The biographies of Joan of Arc are now beyond counting. Their authors include the most illustrious literary figures. The theater and cinema have elaborately portrayed the stirring drama of her life. Those writers who have tried to explain why they chose this subject have done so in poetic and impassioned terms.

Take for instance Gabriel Hanotaux, an outstanding historian and former Foreign Minister of France:

"I didn't choose the subject; it chose me. In my eagerness to know and understand, I approached and admired. After I had studied and reflected, I started to write. That is the genesis of the present work."

More recently, the successful playwright and professed unbeliever, Jean Anouilh, told why, to his mind, we must not try to find any explanation for Joan of Arc:

"There is no more explanation for her than for the little flower that grows by the side of the road. There is a living flower that always knew, even when it was a tiny seed, how many petals it would have and to what size they would grow, and to what precise shade of blue.... There is a phenomenon that is Joan, just as there is a phenomenon-daisy, a phenomenon-bird, a phenomenon-sky. How pretentious can men be, not to be satisfied with that!" (1953)

Quite obviously, Anouilh wanted his words to eliminate any vestige of the supernatural from Joan's story. In the following pages, we shall scrupulously strive to present the simple, naked, historic truth, and yet the supernatural in Joan's life will appear in all its clarity. For the moment, we accept the unbeliever's metaphor: *Joan, a beautiful flower of French history!*

HER BIRTH, HER NAME

Tradition has set January 6, 1412, as the date of Joan's birth. At that time there were no civil records. No reliable document exists to confirm this basic fact, but there could not be any serious error on this point.

As to the place of birth, no doubt is possible. Joan was born at Domremy, a small village that formed a parish with another village, Greux, in the territory of Barrois, a dependency of France, on the border between Champagne and Lorraine. The reason she has so often been called *Joan of Lorraine*, in past times and even in our own day, is because of the uncertainty as to the juridical situation of her native village. Joan was not from Lorraine, for Lorraine was not part of France then. She was and considered herself to be French.

There is a similar confusion about her name. We always call her *Joan of Arc*. But strange to say, she never used this name. It was not yet the custom for a child to take his or her father's "surname." What was then called the "surname" is what we now call the last name, or family name. But Joan never used her father's name, or her mother's, for that matter. She constantly spoke of herself, and was called by her contemporaries, whether friends or enemies, *Jeanne-la-Pucelle,* that is to say, Joan-the-Virgin, Joan-the-Maid consecrated to God.

When she was questioned before the tribunal of Rouen, after being made to kneel and take an oath on the Missal, she answered:

"In my district I was called *Jeannette.* After I came to France, I was called *Jeanne.* I was born in Domremy, which is joined to Greux. The principal church is at Greux.

"My father's name was Jacques Darc; my mother's, Isabelle.

"I was baptized in the church of Domremy.

"My godmothers were named Agnes, Joan, and Sibyl; my godfathers, John Lingué and John Barrey, but my mother told me I had several others besides.

"The priest who baptized me is, I believe; Monsieur John Minet. And I think he's still alive.

"As to my age, I think I'm 19 [it was in 1431, and she was in her twentieth year].

"It was from my mother only that I learned the *Our Father,* the *Hail Mary,* and the *Creed.* No one else ever taught me anything...."

We have many precise details on all these things. The village of Domremy is still there. One can still see and visit the modest cottage where Joan was born and spent her early years.

There is a very small cell, lighted by a single narrow window, that is said to have been her room. The church where she was baptized still stands, not far from her home. It is now a kind of national museum and pilgrimage site. It is still the same externally, but the interior has been changed around. The altar is now where the entrance portal once stood, and vice versa. But it was in this church that Joan prayed, confessed to her pastor, participated in the Holy Sacrifice of the Mass on Sundays and feastdays and often on ordinary weekdays as well. It was here that she received the Body of Jesus Christ, present in the sacred host.

But we are not interested merely in the village. Its inhabitants are of far greater concern to us. It is a rare, indeed a unique fact that we are able, after more than five hundred years, to call to life the inhabitants of the little rural market-town that came to be called *Domremy-la-Pucelle*, because it had been the birthplace of our Joan.

As a rule, villagers are not long remembered by their fellow citizens. The local cemetery does not keep their tombstones intact, and local chronicles do not preserve their memory.

The case of Domremy is different. We can actually name the worthy peasants who lived around Joan during her early years, those she greeted as she passed, those who answered her young girl's greeting with a smile, those who thought, as they saw her: "What a fine girl is this Jeannette!"

The reason is that twenty-five years after Joan's tragic death, they were convoked for the rehabilitation proceedings. The tribunal in charge of the proceedings sent investigators to Domremy, and then to Vaucouleurs. Everyone who had known Joan was summoned to appear personally. They were made to take an oath on the Gospel to tell the whole truth and nothing but the truth. They were carefully informed that anyone guilty of bearing false witness commits several sins. First, he shows scorn for his Creator, the Author of all truth; second, he deceives the judge; and also, he wrongs his neighbor and prepares only for hell by incurring the stain of perpetual infamy.

So this was indeed an impressive parade of witnesses. We can say quite truthfully that there are few if any historical facts so faithfully attested to as those relating to Joan's place of birth, the names and occupations of her parents, what Joan did as a child in the village, how she left her district, and the rest of her story.

More than thirty persons appeared to answer the judges' twelve questions. These included John Morelli; Dominic Jacobi; Beatrice, widow of Estellin; Jeannette, wife of Thévenin; Stephen of Syona; Jeannette, wife of Thiesselin; and many others. Among all these peasants there was even a "nobleman," Louis de Martigny, who was a squire.

The investigators must have been especially pleased to hear the emotional deposition of Gerard of Syona's wife. Her name was Hauviette. She had been one of Joan's most intimate friends, and declared she had not only spent much time with her but had often slept at her house, out of friendship. We shall come back to this reliable testimony later on. We shall also speak of another of Joan's intimate friends, her dear Mangette. When she made her deposition in 1456, she was married to a man named Joyart. She had lived next door to Joan. She had often sat by her side sewing, and had shared various household tasks with her.

We almost feel we know Joan's contemporaries and fellow villagers. We can hear them speak. They live and breathe before us in their depositions before the tribunal of 1456. From their words we can form a true picture of Joan's way of life before she left Domremy.

JOAN'S VARIOUS ACTIVITIES

It should cause us no surprise to discover that nothing set Joan apart from the other girls of her own age and time in her rural home, until the day when heaven itself — we might say — snatched her from her milieu to carry out its plans for France.

All the depositions we have just referred to present Joan as a normal young girl. She lived like all her friends in Domremy. If she was in any way different from the others it was probably by reason of her inward, invisible gifts of more perfect piety, more fervent devotion, greater selflessness and charity to others. But only God knew these things. Joan's holiness, especially at the time of her birth, was a secret between God and her soul.

Let us listen to what John Morelli has to say: "Joan's parents were Jacques [James] Darc and her mother Isabelle. They were husbandmen of Domremy, good and faithful Catholics, good farmers, of good reputation and of honorable conduct, for I have had many contacts with them. I was even one of Joan's godparents."

Second witness: Dominic Jacobi. He was a priest, the pastor of Montiers-en-Salux, in the diocese of Toul. He was younger than Joan, and had seen her only three or four years before she left the village. What he knew of Joan's work was that she followed the plow with her father, watched the animals in the fields, sewed and did other women's tasks at home. He testified to her virtues and devotion.

In the depositions we are studying, one statement recurs several times, namely, that in season and at other times as well, Joan watched the village livestock when it was her father's turn.

To understand what this means, we must remember that in the villages of eastern France, after the harvest the entire expanse of the community's fields served as a kind of pasture for all the animals of the village regardless of their owners, so that every household had its "turn" to watch over the village flock in what they often called the *étendue* or common. When it was the turn of Joan's father, she and perhaps her brothers when they were still quite young and her sister Catherine would watch not only their father's animals but those of the entire peasant community of Domremy.

It is in this sense that we can say she was a "shepherdess." But she was never a shepherdess by profession. Rather, she participated in all the tasks of the house. Her mother had taught her to spin hemp or wool. She herself boasted with a smile that where sewing was concerned she "feared no girl from Rouen," which was renowned for its skilled needle-workers.

She helped her mother and shared in all the housekeeping tasks, sweeping, preparing the meals, and all the rest. When her father was out plowing, she would walk in front of the cows to guide the plow's furrow.

Mangette described it very clearly, as Hauvi-ette had done before her. She said under oath at the tribunal of 1456 that she often sewed with Joan or did other household tasks, in the daytime and evening. For, she added, Joan liked to work, and took care of many things. This means that Joan was never idle. For she was either sewing, doing the housework, and in due season—that is, after the harvest—she watched the animals, as she sat sewing, when it was her turn.

There is no need to insist. If we were to cite all the witnesses from the village, we would simply be repeating ourselves over and over.

So much for Joan's life as others saw it unfold. In the next chapter we shall speak of what must be called her *interior life,* for it was here that her great mission was secretly being prepared. It is worth noting once again that in all that came under human scrutiny, Joan was "just like everybody else" in the village. In other words, she was a healthy and vigor-ous plant, a flower of the fields, a hardworking young girl, active, skillful with her fingers and strong with her hands, a girl who knew how to do, and do very well, everything that came within the province of a woman in the village of her ancestors. There was nothing morbid or abnormal about her, nothing that would offend the eyes or call attention to her.

In the matter of book learning, Joan was like the majority of her rural contemporaries. She was totally ignorant. She herself said that she never learned to read or write, and that—to use her own words—she knew neither "A" nor "B."

It was not in books that she would learn the great deeds we shall see her accomplish later on.

A TROUBLED TIME

To give a complete idea of Joan's concerns and activities as a child in Domremy, we must situate her peaceful, regular life, a life that was both varied and monotonous, within the context of the times. Joan's entire childhood was spent amid rumors of war.

We can form some idea of it by comparing it to our own life in the twentieth century, which has seen two devastating world wars, limited wars, "cold wars." Even without wanting to, and often without realizing it, we breathe air polluted with threats of world catastrophe. In the early fifteenth century the peace of the villages, even Domremy in its remote corner of French territory, was poisoned by maddening rumors of an interminable war, to which historians have given the sinister name of the "Hundred Years' War."

As soon as Jeannette was old enough to know anything, as soon as she could listen to what was being said around her, especially in the evening or during the family meal, she knew that France was a very unhappy nation, that a cruel fate threatened her very existence, that war was raging throughout the kingdom, and that the English were winning victory upon victory over the French.

Her child's heart was crushed when she heard people talk about her country's misfortunes. It would be an error to think that patriotism did not exist in France at that time. In any case, if it had disappeared or lay dormant in the hearts of others, it was very much alive in her own heart, the heart of a true child of France. And yet all she could do at that time was to weep and pray, pray very hard for her country.

Domremy was situated at a crossroads between the north and the south, the east and the west. While there was no public mail service at that time, the princes and towns used special messengers to relay their news and needs to others at a distance. Among the messengers who passed through Domremy were knights carrying various dispatches, mendicant friars, soldiers going in various directions, mercenaries and travelers of all sorts. These travelers would tell the peasants, always eager for news, what they knew — and sometimes even what they didn't know.

What was the condition of France during Joan's early youth?

Three years after she was born, the English had met the French army at Agincourt (1415). The French suffered a total defeat, and lost the flower of their nobility in this disastrous encounter. King Charles VI had been insane since the year 1392. His relatives governed in his stead, jealously and pitilessly tearing each other to pieces. The French were divided into two factions that were mortal enemies: the Armagnacs and the Burgundians. Paris, the capital of France, had been set on fire and drenched in blood by their infernal battles. In 1419, Rouen was taken by the English. The ancient province of Normandy, that the English had claimed since the days of Philip Augustus, had fallen into their hands.

That same year of 1419, the followers of Dauphin Charles massacred John the Fearless, Duke of Burgundy, at the Montereau Bridge, claiming it was simply revenge for a crime in which the Duke of Orleans had perished in 1407.

All these dissensions and misfortunes of France were aggravated by still another fact. By the side of the sick and incompetent monarch lived his queen, who was a foreigner and had not espoused the interests of her adopted land. This was Isabeau of Bavaria, one of the most despicable figures in French history. Not only did she live an unedifying life of luxury and sensuality, but she did not hesitate to disinherit her own son, Dauphin Charles. She did this by signing the shameful Treaty of Troyes in 1420 with the Duke of Burgundy, Philip the Good, son of John the Fearless, which turned France over to England at the death of the reigning king, Charles VI.

That is what did happen. The victor at Agincourt had become the son-in-law of Charles VI and Isabeau of Bavaria through his marriage to Catherine of France. Through this treaty, he became the Regent of the Kingdom of France, which was to come into the hands of his heirs. Burgundy and England were dividing the spoils of the Kingdom of France between themselves. The great work of the Capetians, the coalescers of the French land, was interrupted and threatened with total destruction. Soon there would be no France at all.

When we remember that just a hundred years later an English sovereign, Henry VIII, would create a deplorable schism within the Church, opening the door to heresy, we can imagine the terrible danger that threatened both France and the Catholic Church.

We need to know all these details in order to understand the stakes of the struggle into which little Joan was to be thrown, and the immensity of the task that the little part-time "shepherdess" of Domremy would be called to accomplish. Rarely was it truer that "God...singled out the weak of this world to shame the strong!" (1 Cor. 1:27)

THE "KING OF BOURGES"

We have not yet finished describing the troubles of France, as indeed we must if we are to measure the work of our remarkable heroine.

On August 13, 1422, two years after the Treaty of Troyes, King Henry V of England, who had solemnly entered Paris as a victor two years earlier, died at Vincennes on French soil. Our Jeannette was then only ten years old.

Charles VI died soon afterward, on October 22, without regaining the use of his reason.

The successor to the English king was a new-born infant, Henry VI. In his name, his uncles, the Duke of Bedford and the Cardinal of Winchester, were recognized as tutors and regents during his minority.

Meanwhile, "Dauphin" Charles, who was to become Charles VII, was proclaimed king by his partisans. But he had no means of access to Paris, the capital, or to Rheims, where his claim to kingship had to be confirmed by the ceremony of the anointing and coronation in order to have its full luster in the eyes of Frenchmen. Dauphin Charles was forced to withdraw to the south of the Loire River. He was derisively called "the King of Bourges," because the capital of the province of Berry had become the capital of his kingdom.

Dauphin Charles was disheartened, badly served, almost inactive, and even—it seems—tormented by doubt. As we shall see, one of Joan's missions was to dispel this abominable uncertainty, as a messenger from heaven.

Disaster followed upon disaster. Evidently, the military operations of that age had no resemblance to the warfare of our own time. Armies consisted of relatively few men and they rarely engaged in battle. Even so, the French were always the losers.

On July 13, 1423, there was the defeat of Cravant. On August 17th of the following year, there was the defeat of Verneuil.

Let us keep this date of August 17, 1424, in mind. France seemed to have reached the bottom of the abyss into which it had been falling. But in the distance, unknown to all, in the fields of Domremy a ray of light was beginning to glimmer.

It is certain that in human terms the situation of France was beyond hope. It had to reach this juncture before "the finger of God" could be seen pointing the way.

The "King of Bourges" had now lost more than half of his kingdom. North of the Loire River he had only four strongholds of any importance left: Mont Saint Michel in the west; Tournai in the north; Orleans at the center; and far in the east, Vaucouleurs, a short distance from Domremy.

The commandant of the last-named stronghold was a rough-hewn soldier with whom we shall soon become better acquainted, Robert de Baudricourt. He would have to settle one of the most delicate problems facing the conscience of a leader in time of war.

He would have to expose himself to ridicule by sending a young seventeen-year-old girl to his sovereign as "heaven-sent help," or he would have to shut the door to France's last hope if he sent this young girl away.

To complete this heartrending prospect, let us add that in the year 1425 even Joan's district was rocked by the war of succession in Lorraine. Although as we have said, Joan was not a Lorrainer, her home was so close to the border of Lorraine that the "robbers" and marauders who made up the armies of those days threatened her village as well as all the others in that area.

In such a situation, the inhabitants had only one recourse. They had to gather their flocks in haste, pack up their clothes, and seek refuge in a secure fortress nearby. This is what happened to our Jeannette. Her parents were forced to seek shelter in the neighboring fortified town of Neufchâteau. They remained there for four days, in a state of great apprehension. They were then able to return to their home, but only to find much devastation.

So we see that *Jeanne-la-Pucelle* or Joan-the-Virgin, grew up in a time heavy with catastrophe.

In the next chapter we shall see how and why she came to take this name, which, in her language and in the usage of the time had a religious meaning which was very precise and very significant.

France, lost by a woman, was to be saved by a virgin!

2

The Voices

We have waited until this chapter to talk about what we have called rather ambitiously Joan's "interior life." And yet that is the only appropriate expression. Interior life begins with prayer. The moment a child prays, addresses himself in his heart to his God, that is, to an invisible but all-powerful, all-loving, omnipresent Being who knows everything, sees everything, hears every petition — at that moment there is a beginning of interior life. Indeed, this sacred dialogue between the soul and its Creator goes on deep within the person, far from the eyes of others. No human eye can see, even less can it measure, the direction of this deep aspiration, its intensity, sweetness, fervor, or the love that is beginning to burgeon in a soul.

Like all Catholic children, Joan had learned to pray at her mother's knee.

Nowadays we know that mothers sometimes forget to teach their children to pray, and the reason is too often that they themselves don't pray any more. That is one of the most telling signs and perhaps one of the causes of present-day spiritual decadence. God abandons only those who have first turned away from Him.

Isabelle Romée had early taught her daughter Joan to join her little hands while devoutly saying the sweet name of Jesus. It was a custom of rural France. A little later Joan learned to recite the most beautiful and ordinary Christian prayers: the *Our Father*, that matchless pearl which one of the Fathers of the Church rightly called the summary of the entire Gospel. Then she learned the *Hail Mary*, or Angelic salutation, which calls to mind the dawn of our redemption. And finally she learned the *Apostles' Creed*, or summing up of the Catholic faith.

These prayers had found deep response in the child's heart. She felt as though she had always known them. We might almost say that, although she didn't know it, they were in her blood. It is thought Isabelle had been given the name of Romée because of the pilgrimages she had made, and in those days they were serious and dangerous undertakings. So little Joan had a fine example to follow in her mother's devotion.

The village church was dedicated to Saint Remigius, and the name of the village, *Domremy,* is the equivalent of Saint-Rémy, or St. Remigius. As we have already said, the church was close to the Darc cottage. Only the cemetery which surrounded the church separated them. When Joan was still a tiny girl she would go to church, clinging to her mother's skirts, and she would gaze at the stained glass windows, which some have called the "bible" of the illiterate. She would see the figures of the saints depicted on them. She was taught very early to turn her eyes toward the tabernacle where, she was told, the Child Jesus was really present.

We have no details on Joan's first Holy Communion. At that time, the children of the parish didn't receive their first Communion together on a special, solemn day. Each child received Communion at his parents' side, on a date set by them and by the pastor of the parish.

We can really say that the only "first" Communion was a private one. The practice of solemn

"First Communion" was instituted much later in Ursuline boarding schools, early in the seventeenth century.*

One thing seems almost certain. From the day Joan received Communion at her mother's side for the first time, she probably received Communion on all the principal feasts of the liturgical year. In any case, she never missed Sunday Mass, and participated in the Holy Sacrifice with all the fervor of her young heart.

There is another detail we have learned from her own revelations, and that is the sweet delight she felt when the church bells rang the *Angélus*. This prayer had just recently spread throughout the Christian world. It had been started at the end of the thirteenth century, when it was said only in the evening. In fact, dusk had come to be called "the Angelus," because of this practice. During the fourteenth century, the ringing of the church bells in the morning was also added. And finally in Joan's time, people were beginning to recite the Angelus at noon as well.

Wherever she might be, when Joan heard the sound of the bells she would get on her knees and pray fervently.

SUPERSTITION?

During the Rouen Trial, efforts would be made to accuse Joan of superstitious practices. One of the hideous tricks of the trial was to charge her with the shameful crime of witchcraft. To this end, mention was made of certain local traditions prevalent at Domremy as in many other places. Those who know the pagan customs prior to the conversion of France to Christianity know that the Gaulish peasants addressed their worship less to wise gods than to vegetable and animal beings and natural phenomena such as a large tree, a spring, a beautiful lake, etc.

---

*Translator's note: It is interesting that the trend now is precisely toward the practice of family First Communion as in the days of St. Joan of Arc in the 1400's.

If we read the sermons of St. Caesar of Arles given in the sixth century, we can readily understand how widespread these superstitions to very beautiful trees had been among the Gauls and how hard it had been to uproot them. As it happened, there was a magnificent beech tree at Domremy that was called the "Beautiful May," and it grew near a spring called the spring of the "currant bushes." At certain times of year the people of Domremy came there to hold little celebrations. It seems they attributed healing powers for fevers to the waters of the spring.

About a mile and a quarter from Domremy stood a splendid oak forest, called *Bois-Chesnu*, or "Oakwood."

It was said that a prophecy attributed to Merlin the magician, but also to the Venerable Bede and to the Sybil, foretold that a "virgin" would come to save the Kingdom of France.

That was all very vague, nebulous, and uncertain. Joan was grilled over and over again about these matters by her judges in Rouen. And she answered with her customary simplicity that all she knew about all those things was what she had heard the people of the village tell. She added that she had gone with the other children of the village to play at "the feast of the Fountains" and had placed garlands of flowers on "Beautiful May." But she had never seen "fairies" and didn't believe what people said about them. She really believed only what was said and done at church. She also liked to make pilgrimages to Notre-Dame de Bermont, not far from her village.

All in all, we wonder if Joan's contemporaries really believed in fairies, or whether this was not a kind of legend for them, similar to our modern-day Santa Claus, whom we tell our children about until they are too big to believe in him any more.

As for Joan, no one was ever able to convince her to put any credence in such superstitions. In this, she was like the other normal, clearheaded young girls of her own age and time.

Nevertheless, Joan would be convicted at Rouen as a witch and a relapsed heretic. How could such an accusation be made against her?

The judges used the device of turning what she called her "Voices" against her. And they tried to make her say that she believed more in her "Voices" than in the legitimate authority of the Church.

We must, therefore, turn our attention to the fact of Joan's "Voices."

JOAN'S "VOICES"

On this point, Joan never wavered. She always affirmed that whatever she had done she had done at the command of her "Voices." So we see she acknowledged the influence of forces superior to the ordinary events that fill most human lives. She claimed she received commands from heaven. She had experienced, and continued to experience, *apparitions.* And while these were not always *visions,* at least they were always *auditions,* that is to say, "Voices."

We cannot dodge this extraordinary fact. Without her Voices, Joan was nothing. She was just an ordinary girl, like everybody else. Without the Voices there would have been no "Joan of Arc Case," or to use her own words, no *Cas Jeanne-la-Pucelle,* that is, no "Joan-the-Virgin Case."

It was by heeding her Voices that she became the liberator of history, and ultimately, a canonized saint.

It is most important, therefore, that we clarify this question of Joan's Voices. Only those who have already made up their minds one way or the other can refuse to examine it carefully.

HOW THEY WERE UNIQUE

First of all, Joan's Voices were in a sense very different from other apparitions known to history.

There have certainly been apparitions to which we can and should give credence in good faith. For instance, the apparitions of the Sacred Heart to the Visitation nun, Margaret Mary Alacoque, at Paray-le-Monial; more recently, the apparitions of the Blessed Virgin Mary to the Sister of Charity, Catherine Labouré; the apparition of the Weeping Virgin at La Salette; the eighteen apparitions of our Lady to Bernadette Soubirous at Lourdes; and likewise the apparitions of Mary to the shepherd children of Fatima. All of these apparitions have been considered authentic, after due investigation by ecclesiastical authorities.

But Joan-the-Virgin's Voices differ in at least one aspect from all the other apparitions we have just mentioned. This difference lies in their continuation over a considerable period of time and also in their frequency. Joan of Arc was enlightened, instructed, consoled, encouraged, and guided by her Voices for at least six years of her short life, and perhaps seven.

We do not know the exact date when she first heard them, but it could not have been later than the summer of 1425, and it was very probably the summer of 1424, until her death by burning in 1431.

HOW THE VOICES BEGAN

The best we can do is tell the story very simply of how Joan's Voices influenced her life.

She herself revealed in the presence of her judges at Rouen what she had never said in detail to anyone, except perhaps to King Charles VII. She declared that she had first heard her Voices when she was about thirteen years old. As she was born on January 6, 1412, she entered her thirteenth year on January 6, 1424. So it must have been early in the summer of 1424 when this event first occurred that was to continue without interruption until her death.

She was out in the fields, watching the cattle and sheep, as we have explained earlier. If the harvest was already in, which was probably not the case, she was watching the flocks of the entire village. If not, she was watching her father's flock only. Artistic conceptions of her usually show her at this moment surrounded by a few sheep.

Suddenly a boy came running toward her and shouted from afar:

"Jeannette! Go home. Your mother needs you!"

Then the boy disappeared.

Joan rushed home, like the obedient daughter she was. Her mother was surprised to see her and told her that she had not sent for her. Somebody must have wanted to play a joke on her, as often happens among children.

Joan then left the cottage and walked into the garden, on the side of the cemetery and the church. At that precise moment the noon *Angelus* rang out. Much later, in a deposition before her judges, she declared that on the eve of that particular day she had fasted, no doubt in a spirit of penance. Had this been an inspiration from above? Or perhaps had she wanted to do something special as a mark of reverence for Friday, the day Christ died? The reason we refer to Friday is this: It seems that at the time Joan lived, and up to the middle of the fifteenth century, that is, until the papacy of Callistus III, it was only on Fridays that the *Angelus* was rung at noon. It was, of course, rung morning and evening every day of the week. In any case, right after Joan had devoutly recited the noonday *Angelus*, all of a sudden she heard a voice from the direction of the church calling her name very distinctly:

"Jeannette! Jeannette!"

She was shaken to the depths of her being. Then she turned instinctively in the direction of the church, where this gentle voice seemed to originate. She saw a great light that seemed to envelop her, and within the light she saw a noble and gentle face, surrounded by a multitude of celestial beings.

Then the same voice that had called out to her said:

"Jeannette! Jeannette! Be good and wise; love God very much. Go to church often!"

The first time she heard her Voices, Joan later confessed, she had been terrified. She could not understand what was happening to her. And yet, a great peace seemed to fill her soul. She felt she was a better person. Besides, the extraordinary idea came to her—extraordinary indeed for one so young —to consecrate herself totally to God by a vow of *perpetual virginity*. From that day on, she was to think of herself as *Jeanne-la-Pucelle*, Joan-the-Virgin, consecrated to God and to His service. Gradually, everyone else who came in contact with her would call her *Jeanne-la-Pucelle*, too.

WHAT WERE THESE VOICES?

This first apparition was to be followed by many others. Later on, Joan was to say she heard her Voices two or three times a week. That went on from 1424 to 1429, and then the visitations increased in frequency.

During this first or what might be called "preparatory" phase, it seems there were one hundred to one hundred and fifty apparitions a year, or a total of some five hundred to seven hundred and fifty over a period of five years. It is because of their great number that Joan's apparitions were different from all others known to history.

The Rouen Trial has provided extensive information on the Voices themselves, on the supernatural personages who appeared to Joan and spoke to her, and on the nature of her conversations with them. Her judges interrogated her repeatedly on this aspect of her mission. This should not surprise us. Obviously, they did so out of their underlying hostility against her and with a rancor that horrifies us. But they had correctly understood that here was the key to the whole mystery of *Jeanne-la-Pucelle*.

If Joan's Voices were from God, then the king's enemies were wrong. At all costs, the judges had to prove that these Voices could only come from the devil. Most, if not all, of the judges were what we would nowadays call "collaborators." They had accepted the yoke of the enemy, and they were working for the victory of the English. Joan's justification would have been their condemnation.

But long before the trial at Rouen, Joan had been placed under scrutiny by a commission of inquiry before the King of France, Charles VII, would accept her services. This commission had convened at Poitiers in March and April, 1429. And there, too, she had been pressed with questions about her Voices. It reminds us of the way Bernadette was questioned about the Lourdes apparitions by an episcopal commission many centuries later (1858). Joan kept asking her judges to refer to the records of the Poitiers inquiry. Unfortunately, these records were never found.

We must therefore rely on what Joan said at Rouen. There again we are sure to hear the echo of her Voices, for she said she always consulted them whenever she was to appear before the tribunal.

"Do you hear your Voices here?" she was asked.

"Yes, I hear them...."

"And what are they telling you?..."

"They tell me to answer fearlessly!..."

And that's just what she did.

WHOSE VOICES?

One point on which Joan never changed her story was with regard to who her heavenly visitors were.

She admitted she didn't know right away who was speaking to her. But by the third apparition she knew it was an angel. Soon she realized this angel was none other than St. Michael, patron of France.

And from the start St. Michael announced to her that he would bring women saints to her, and these saints appeared to her very often. They were St. Margaret and St. Catherine.

Another point on which Joan never had the slightest doubt was that her Voices were from God. Indeed, they told her only to live a good life, pray fervently, go to confession and Communion regularly.

Theologians would probably compare these consoling and elevating apparitions to what is sometimes called "passive prayer." For a time, Jeannette was even carried up into the midst of the angels by an unknown force. She felt a strong attraction to a life of personal holiness. When she came away from her heavenly conversations, she always did so with a sense of courage, confidence, devotion, and—as we shall soon show—humility.

THE POWER OF THE VOICES

These experiences were in some ways like the actual graces that every fervent Christian receives, and yet they were different. What was the same was the healthy and sanctifying impulse they gave to Joan's life. Every genuine prayer creates such an effect, whether consciously or not. In fact, more often than not we are not even aware of it.

Jesus Christ has said: *"Ask and you will receive"* (Mt. 7:7). We are certain, therefore, that our prayers are answered. Our good thoughts, our yearning for holiness, the inspirations that come to us from God are the ordinary fruit of our prayers. These are actual graces. In Joan's case, her Voices had the same effects, but in a much more intense degree. But grace flowed into Joan's heart by more direct channels. She could actually see actual grace come to her, if we dare say so, in the form of her saint friends, and through St. Michael.

In a word, we don't see who is speaking to us, but Joan did.

As she said at Rouen: "I saw them with my bodily eyes, just as well as I see you. And when they would go away [referring to St. Michael and his angels], I wept and wished they would take me away with them."

These are stirring and revealing words, like so many others Joan uttered.

Another question that was asked of her was whether all these angels looked alike.

"Some of them did indeed look alike," she answered, "and others didn't, as I saw them. There were some wearing crowns, and others without crowns. There were some, too, with St. Catherine and St. Margaret. And at Chinon there were angels even in the king's chamber...."

On another occasion, the judges wanted to know how her Voices addressed her.

Joan answered: "They would say to me: *daughter of God, daughter of the Church, great-hearted daughter.* But later on, when I was in France, before the raising of the siege of Orleans, and every day afterwards, they often called me: *Jeanne-la-Pucelle, daughter of God!*"

A GREAT SECRET

One thing that deserves particular attention on our part is the secrecy which Joan maintained about the divine favors lavished upon her. We have already mentioned her humility. It is a universally accepted fact in the Church that there is no holiness without humility. But what better word can we use to describe Joan's reserve on the subject of her Voices than to call it humility?

Here was a thirteen-year-old child. She was full of life, cheerful, and a hard worker. She had several very close friends, Hauviette, Mangette, and doubtless others. She had parents she loved and revered, and whom it cost her dearly to leave. She had a pastor in her parish to whom she went to confession regularly.

Would not anyone forgive this young girl if she had let a few words slip to her companions, if she had confided in her mother, her pastor, about the extraordinary things that were happening to her? But she did no such thing! She spoke to no one, not even to her pastor, or to her beloved parents, and even less to her companions at play or work.

Never, perhaps, was so great a secret so well guarded. At Lourdes, Bernadette couldn't keep her secret for even an hour. Joan kept hers for five years, without faltering, and what is even more significant, without any explicit command from above. When she was questioned on this point by her judges at Rouen, she answered very categorically.

The text of the trial says: "When interrogated as to whether she ever spoke about her visions to her pastor or to any Churchman: answers no, but only to Robert de Baudricourt and to her king. And says, moreover, that she was not constrained to hide it by her Voices; but she hesitated greatly to reveal it, out of fear of the Burgundians—the enemies of her king—and that they would prevent her journey. And especially was afraid of her father, that he would be opposed to her departure."

In the manuscript published by Quicherat (1, 128), a marginal note in Latin reads: "She hid her visions from the pastor, from her father and her mother, and from everybody."

So there was no pride on her part in seeing she had been chosen by God. No inclination to boast, to seek her own glory, or even to make more or less veiled allusions to such a weighty secret.

Certainly, she gave as reasons that she feared to alert either her father or the Burgundians, which could have resulted in preventing her journey, at least for the last period of the apparitions. But these reasons were not valid at the start when the

Voices had not yet spoken to Joan of France and its misfortunes, and of the mission that would be entrusted to her, a little peasant girl, to save France.

Such a silence from the beginning on Joan's part, without any express obligation, is indeed remarkable. The seers of La Salette, Bernadette, and the shepherds of Fatima had all received a clear command to remain silent. Joan's voluntary silence, therefore, reveals her good common sense, restraint, self-mastery, and, above all, a humility, an absence of pride and boastfulness, an indifference to praise that stirs our admiration.

TWO PHASES

It will be helpful to distinguish two very distinct phases in the revelations made to Joan. In the first period there was no question yet between her and her Voices of anything but her own spiritual progress. Nothing was said to her about France. In one form or another the Voices often came back to the formula of the first day:

"Jeannette, Jeannette! Be good and wise, be good and pious, go to church often!"

This was a preparatory phase. Joan's apparitions, as in the case of all who have been favored with them through the centuries, were *free gifts, charisms,* that were not intended for her alone. God had chosen her for a unique task in the history of France and almost in the history of mankind. The Voices were preparing her long in advance for this task.

That is the way of Providence. Mary, the Mother of God, had been prepared from the moment of her conception. Obviously, Joan's mission was in no sense comparable to that of the Mother of God. But she, too, needed to be prepared, and to be prepared long in advance. These encouragements, these heavenly inspirations, must certainly have given Joan the gentleness, piety, charity to the poor and sick, that witnesses were to attest to at the Rehabilitation proceedings.

But a second phase was to follow this preparation. A day came, which we cannot pinpoint because Joan didn't do it for us, when her Voices spoke to her, to use her own stirring and immortal words, *"of the great pity that exists in the Kingdom of France."*

But here again, everything did not happen all at once. Providence was carefully preparing the way for the transition. The Voices spoke to the child of a great hope. Joan understood that God had not abandoned the country she loved so well. France would be saved. If the angel of victory, St. Michael, had come to see her, it was surely a sign that victory was near.

Joan thanked her Voices for this good news. She probably made bold to ask for a few details, and expressed the desire to know the name of her country's savior. Then, and only then, did the mystery become clear.

The heavenly messenger declared to her, in one way or another, that she was the chosen one.

"It's you, daughter of God!... It's you who will liberate France!... Leave! Go to France! You must!..."

THE STRUGGLE

Then a struggle broke loose that can only be called the battle between Joan and her Voices.

What they were asking of her was so extraordinary, so far beyond her strength, that it made her tremble in every fiber of her being. She began to sob.

"I am only a poor girl!" she said with great anguish. "I don't know how to ride a horse or to make war...."

But the Archangel sank an arrow into her heart, and repeated once more before leaving her:

"Leave! Leave! Go to France! You must!"

The child remained overwhelmed, dismayed. She didn't doubt, but she could not understand why heaven had chosen her. Her humility shone forth in all its truth. She knew she was nothing; she knew she was powerless.

And it was precisely her weakness that had brought God's choice upon her.

"I am only a poor girl, and know neither 'A' nor 'B'! I can't ride a horse, or make war!"

What she said was all too true. She was not mistaken on this point. But the Voices would not let her rest. She must leave. She would some day say before her judges that she became very restless. It was stronger than she was; she had to go.

JACQUES DARC'S DREAM

Meanwhile, a very strange thing happened. Joan's father, who couldn't have known anything about the Voices, had a dream. In his dream he saw a woman marching at the head of an army, and he recognized this woman to be his own daughter.

This upset him so much that the next morning he told his wife about it. He couldn't help thinking of those degraded women who were sometimes seen in the company of mercenaries, and so he added:

"If I were sure this was going to happen, I'd tell Jeannette's brothers to drown her, and if they wouldn't obey, then I'd drown her with my own hands!"

Joan learned from her mother about her father's dream and his reaction to it. This was certainly not calculated to give her the extraordinary courage she needed to obey her Voices.

And yet the Voices continued to urge her to leave:

"Leave," they would say to her. *"God will help you!"*

Later on, when Joan was telling the king about it at Chinon, she said that finally the Voices had overcome her resistance with the words:

"Daughter of God, go, go, go. I will be your helper. Go!"

And so she set out.

3

Toward
Vaucouleurs

DURAND LAXART

When Providence gives someone a mission to carry out, it does not always eliminate every obstacle or open new paths all at once. On the contrary, difficulties often tend to pile up and block the way.

Joan's Voices kept telling her:

"*Fille Dé—daughter of God—go, go, go!*"

But go where?

And by what road?

Humanly speaking, it was absolutely impossible for this seventeen-year-old peasant girl to try to leave her village without being stopped by her family, without arousing the anger of her loving father, who could not tolerate the thought that her virginal honor might be endangered.

Later on, Joan was to say:

"Even if I had to wear my legs down to the knees, I would have gone!"

And these heroic words give us some idea of the force of God's calls, and of her supernatural energy.

But the hardest part was to get out of Domremy in the first place, and then to know where to go.

When everything was obscure on these two points, a light shone in the darkness. At that moment appeared the man whom Providence had chosen to get Joan on her way.

This man was Durand Laxart. He hadn't the vaguest idea what had been going on. But what human beings call *chance* and Christians call *Providence* brought him to Domremy early in 1429 or toward the end of 1428.

Durand Laxart appeared before the Rehabilitation tribunal. He is cited in the Proceedings as the twenty-fifth witness heard by the investigators who had come to Domremy and Vaucouleurs. On January 31, 1456, at Vaucouleurs, he declared that he lived at Burey-le-Petit, not far from Vaucouleurs, that he was sixty years old—or thereabouts—and was sworn in.

During his deposition he explained that Joan was a relative of his wife, who was also named Joan.

He had known Joan's parents, Jacques Darc and Isabelle, very well. He said they were good and faithful Catholics. As to Joan, she was a good girl, devout, patient, liked to go to church, went to confession often, and gave alms to the poor as generously as she could. He had seen her in action in all these aspects of her life, both at Domremy and in his own house at Burey where she had stayed six weeks. She worked energetically, sewed, followed the plow, tended the farm animals, and did other women's work creditably.

Durand said that it was he who came to get Joan at her father's house, to take her to his home.

He needed her help because his young wife was soon expecting a baby. So what happened to Joan was a little like what had happened to the Virgin Mary right after the great mystery of the Annunciation, when she went in haste to her cousin Elizabeth to help her in childbirth.

Joan eagerly seized the opportunity to leave her village, although she had no idea how far it would take her.

She quickly collected a few belongings, and bade brief farewells to a few of her friends whom she passed as she was leaving.

She would never see Domremy again.

A PORTRAIT

One phase of Joan's short earthly life was coming to a close. She was setting out for her great, her divine adventure.

I cannot resist the pleasure of citing the word picture Gabriel Hanotaux has given us of Joan at this precise moment of her life. Obviously, it is purely the work of his imagination, for we have no authentic portrait of our heroine. But it does seem safe to picture her in the following way:

"She was seventeen to eighteen years old, a beautiful girl, tall and strong, with a rounded neck, ...a smiling face, thick black hair. She spoke little but easily, in a gentle and womanly voice. She was well-balanced, chaste, pious, always cheerful, quick, determined, and prompt, without hesitation and without fear, but reserved and prudent, bold yet restrained. She had the ascendancy over men that superior souls exercise. Such was the extraordinary girl, the 'little shepherdess,' who was leaving the village of her birth to save the kingdom of France."

THE SECRET REVEALED

Until this moment Joan had not revealed to a living soul the great secret she was guarding in her heart.

But once on the road to Burey-le-Petit, she could stand it no longer. She spoke to her relative Durand, whom she called "my uncle" because of his age. Actually, Durand was thirty-three years old when she was seventeen.

Their conversation turned to the misfortunes of war and the dangers threatening France. Together they wept over the misfortunes of their country. And suddenly Joan told her stupefied "uncle" that the Archangel Michael had appeared to her, that he had made her understand "the great pity of the kingdom," that saints had also appeared to her, that the kingdom would only be saved by a virgin.

"No," she would keep saying. "No, nothing is lost! God will come to our help. A woman was our ruin; a woman is going to save us!"

And she concluded:

"This woman is a virgin of our district. I'm the one the saints and the Archangel have chosen. I'm the one to whom they said: *'Fille de Dieu, va, va, va!'*"

We don't know just what Joan and Durand said on that occasion. But one thing is certain: Durand Laxart was stunned at first, and probably distrustful, wondering in terror whether his "niece" were losing her mind. But in the end he was won over. She had given him so many precise and luminous details. She was so obviously good, devout, sincere, endowed with common sense, prudence and courage, that he finally agreed to help her in every way he could.

We don't know where the idea to go and see Robert de Baudricourt originated. He was the Provost of the royal fortress of Vaucouleurs. Did Durand think of it, or had Joan received it from her Voices? But it seemed like a good idea to both. Only Robert de Baudricourt could provide an escort and issue orders to have Joan led to the man she called "Dauphin Charles."

According to the deposition, Durand intimated that Joan was the one who had asked him to go to Vaucouleurs. But he could very well have suggested it to her, and she could have accepted it as the wisest course under the circumstances.

Be this as it may, Durand went to Vaucouleurs.

ROBERT DE BAUDRICOURT

It was no easy matter to be admitted into the presence of the Provost. A military leader of his importance, and especially at a time such as this, had to be a tough man, not given to polite niceties.

As we might have expected, when Robert de Baudricourt heard what Durand Laxart had to say about his "niece," he probably burst out laughing or answered a few cutting words, such as:

"This girl is crazy. Someone should box her ears and send her home to her father!"

Durand Laxart said in his deposition that Robert told him several times to take her back to her father's house and give her a few good slaps.

Some historians believe that this first effort occurred in the spring of 1428, and that Joan did in fact return to Domremy for a few months. The chronology of that period of Joan's life is so vague that this might indeed have happened. However, it is not contained in Laxart's deposition of 1456.

On the contrary, Laxart said he then took his "niece" on the pilgrimage of St. Nicholas, with a passport, to the Duke of Lorraine at Nancy. He reported that the duke gave her *four francs*, which was a princely gift in those days, equivalent to about eighty modern American dollars.

In the end, Durand brought Joan back to Vaucouleurs, where a very touching and enthusiastic support was expressed for the young girl.

AT THE ROYERS' HOME

We can cite another and equally precious witness here, that of Catherine, wife of Le Royer, of Vaucouleurs. Her deposition followed immediately after Durand Laxart's.

She said: "When Joan decided to leave her home, she lived with us for about three weeks." During this period efforts were made to get Robert de Baudricourt to change his mind. But Robert would not budge an inch.

Many meetings were held at Vaucouleurs about Joan's case. Some of the soldiers took her side. Joan was gaining ground. Bertrand de Poulengy and John de Metz, who belonged to the Vaucouleurs garrison, were among the first to be won over. One of the burghers, Jacques Alain, also declared himself for her. The pastor of the town, John Fournier, heard her confession. But even so, according to Mistress Le Royer, he arrived at her home one day to exorcise Joan. Robert de Baudricourt was present. The priest put on his stole and sprinkled her with holy water, summoning her to move away from them if she was "evil," but to come close to them if she was "good." Then, says our witness, Joan dragged herself on her knees up to the priest.

After the ceremony of exorcism, Joan declared that the priest had not acted fairly toward her, since he had already heard her confession.

Meanwhile, Robert de Baudricourt continued to hesitate.

It was then that Joan announced to Baudricourt that the French armies had just suffered a new defeat near Orleans. This was the defeat of Rouvray. The Provost noted what Joan said, and when the event was confirmed to him a few days later, he no longer doubted. He offered Joan a sword and gave orders to make her ready for her journey to the Dauphin's residence.

PREPARATIONS

We can easily imagine the excitement in the little fortress of Vaucouleurs, on the border of Lorraine, when it was learned that the Provost had agreed to send this seventeen-year-old girl to see the king.

Everybody crowded around her. They wanted to see her, hear her speak, touch her clothes. People would repeat the things she said. Her hostess, Mistress Le Royer, reported she had been most impressed by what Joan herself had said:

"Have you not heard that it has been prophesied France would be lost by a woman, but that it would be restored by a virgin from the marshes of Lorraine?"

This was one of Joan's favorite affirmations. She repeated it often. Mistress Le Royer attested that she was astounded to hear these words, because she had indeed heard the prophecy.

When the time for Joan's departure finally came, there was much bustling throughout the town to get her properly equipped. She insisted, and it was generally agreed upon, that she could not leave dressed as a woman. The inhabitants of the town got together to provide her with a man's suit of armor and all the equipment needed by a knight going to war: tunic, shoes, shin-guards, a sword, and all the rest.

Jacques Alain and Durand Laxart bought her a cavalry horse for the sum of *twelve francs* — equivalent in modern money to two hundred and forty American dollars. Robert de Baudricourt later reimbursed them for their expense.

The Provost provided Joan with an escort of soldiers who were absolutely loyal and dependable. History has preserved their names, and we must make their acquaintance.

According to the deposition of Durand Laxart, these soldiers were: John de Metz, Bertrand de Poulengy, Colet de Vienne, an archer named Richard, and two servants in the service of Metz and Poulengy respectively.

John de Metz was then in his prime. When he appeared before the investigators of the Rehabilitation proceedings, on the same day as Durand Laxart, January 31, 1456, he claimed he was about fifty-seven years old. So, in 1429, he had been about thirty.

John de Metz told the tribunal that when he met Joan at the Le Royer home, he expressed his concern at the delay in her plans for departure, and said to her:

"Friend, what are you doing here? Must the king be driven out of his kingdom and must we become English?"

"I have come to this royal city," Joan answered, "to speak with Robert de Baudricourt, so that he will have me taken to the king. But he pays no attention to me or to my words. And yet before mid-Lent I must be in the king's presence, even if I have to wear my legs down to the knees! Nobody in the world, neither kings, nor dukes, nor the daughter of the King of Scotland, nor anyone else can reconquer the kingdom of France. I'm the only one who can. I'd much rather stay with my poor mother, because this isn't my calling. But I have to go because my Lord wants me to."

"And who is your Lord?" the soldier retorted.

"It is God!"

"Then," John de Metz said in his deposition, "I gave her my word, by tapping in her hand, that under God's guidance I would lead her to the king. And as I was asking her when she wanted to leave, she said to me:

"'Better today than tomorrow, and better tomorrow than later!'"

John de Metz was later raised to the ranks of the nobility by Charles VII for the faithful services he rendered to *Jeanne-la-Pucelle*.

The second man-at-arms was Bertrand de Poulengy. We also have a deposition from him, dated February 6, 1456. He said he was then about sixty-three years old. Thus, he was six years older than John de Metz.

According to him, Robert de Baudricourt had also asked Joan in his presence the same question John de Metz had asked her:

"And who is your Lord?"

"The King of heaven!" Joan had answered.

Bertrand and John immediately agreed to take Joan to the king. They were in agreement, too, to have her change from her bright woman's clothing to man's attire.

Bertrand insisted on a delicate matter in his deposition. He said that although he was a young man at the time, Joan inspired such respect in him and his companions that no impure intentions ever crossed his mind, even when Joan lay by his side at night on the journey, asleep deep inside her coat of mail.

We know very little about the third man-at-arms, Colet de Vienne. He seems to have played a subordinate role. We have no deposition from him in the Rehabilitation proceedings of 1456.

The same is true of Richard, the archer.

As to the two servants who completed Joan's escort, we know that John de Metz' servant was John de Honecourt, and Bertrand de Poulengy's was named Julian.

THE DEPARTURE

When everything was ready, the little band departed amid an enthusiastic and confident crowd. Although Joan had never ridden a horse, she jumped on her charger with grace and skill. And when the small group of six men led by Joan-the-Virgin got under way, Robert de Baudricourt called out to her with great emotion:

"Go, go, and happen what may!"

We can surmise that even the slightest rumors emanating from Joan's exploits in this land of her birth must have been received with great enthusiasm.

4

Toward
Chinon
and Poitiers

Even for horsemen accustomed to the hard riding of those days, the journey from Vaucouleurs to Chinon, Dauphin Charles' residence, was no small venture. It was a journey of about three hundred seventy-five miles on dangerous roads and through territory held by the Burgundian party, who were allies of the English and enemies of the King of France.

Not only was the area ravaged by war, it was also overrun by bands of pillagers who were often simply disbanded soldiers. There were streams to cross. In principle, the bridges were under military guard. Bertrand de Poulengy cited in his deposition that the men who formed Joan's escort were not very sure of themselves, despite their show of bravery.

According to Bertrand: "The first day, after leaving their own district, they were very much afraid because the Burgundian and English soldiers occupied the area they were crossing. They galloped a whole night through on their mounts." *Jeanne-la-Pucelle*—this was the name she would use from then on—told Poulengy and John de Metz, as well as her other traveling companions, that it would be a good thing for all of them to attend Mass. But so long as they remained in enemy territory this was impossible, lest Joan be recognized by the enemy. "And they were on the road eleven days."

During this long horseback journey, which would have exhausted energies less extraordinary than Joan's, they were often concerned about their safety and had many alerts. But Joan paid no attention to her own fatigue or to the threatening dangers, and kept telling them "not to be afraid."

DIVINE REASSURANCE

Who can fail to admire this superhuman certitude? Nothing had yet been accomplished. For the moment, Joan was only beginning her comet-like career. If she had not been sustained by divine power, we ask any serious-minded reader, how could she have successfully completed an undertaking so far beyond the physical, mental, and spiritual capacities of a seventeen-year-old girl?

A journey on horseback lasting eleven days! That alone would have sufficed to break her courage, had it not been miraculously nourished from above. Eleven days of danger, of extraordinary exhaustion, of nights spent in military armor.

We can readily understand why Gabriel Hanotaux, a historian, a thinker, and a man of experience, felt impelled to write:

"And so, from the start, the account of this life enters the realm of the miraculous: the miracle of the mission, and the miracle of its accomplishment. She declared her proof would consist in the facts...."

And so it would always be for Joan.

When the theologians of Poitiers, who had been ordered to examine her, asked her for a "sign," she answered pluckily:

"In the name of God, I haven't come to Poitiers to give *signs*. But lead me to Orleans, and I'll show you the *sign* for which I have come."

Orleans was the reason for her journey. Orleans, besieged by the English; Orleans, one of the last ramparts of a mutilated France that still obeyed Charles VII; Orleans, threatened with capture by the English. It was, above all else, to deliver Orleans that Joan had come.

THE ARRIVAL

Joan and her escort had left Vaucouleurs on February 23, 1429. On March 5th they reached Sainte-Catherine-de-Fierbois. St. Catherine was very dear to Joan, for she was one of "her saints," the other being St. Margaret. It was a great joy for her to make her pilgrimage and be able to attend three Masses there.

She also wanted to announce her imminent visit to the king, and dictated the following letter to him:

"I have traveled 150 leagues [372 miles] to come and bring you my help. I have many very great things to reveal to you. As proof of what I claim, I shall recognize you from everybody else!"

And she had her signature placed at the bottom of her letter: *Jeanne-la-Pucelle.*

She had no fear of proposing to Dauphin Charles a very easy and simple test. He had only to hide among his courtiers. She claimed she would recognize him without ever having seen him, and this would be a peremptory proof of her supernatural gifts.

Finally, on March 6th at noon, the envoys of Baudricourt arrived at Chinon. Joan was given lodging in the home of a townslady. There she prepared to present herself to the king.

CHARLES VII

Joan called Charles VII "Dauphin Charles," because she found it unfitting to call a man "King" who had not been anointed and crowned. Charles VII was born in Paris in 1403, and was then twenty-six years of age. He had been driven from his capital through the disastrous intrigues of a mother devoid of pity and virtue. He had been forced to withdraw before the English invasion time after time. Having neither a regular army nor finances, nor any serious military alliance, he gradually lost even the hope of recovering his kingdom. Moreover, he was not a model of forcefulness or intellect, but lived very extravagantly, and tried to forget his misfortunes in a round of pleasures. He was surrounded by rapacious counselors, who jealously fought over his meager favors.

Beyond all that, it seems this prince had been tormented by a terrible doubt up to the time of Joan's visit. Was he the legitimate heir to the kingdom? And was he even a legitimate son? He felt the reverses he had suffered—his repudiation by an unworthy mother—were signs that heaven had abandoned him. Perhaps he didn't have any rights at all to the crown that he was claiming as the presumed son of Charles VI.

In any event, all these clouds soon vanished, like snow in the sunshine, when Joan came into the picture.

Almost as soon as she arrived, she made an official request for an audience.

Some of the king's advisers recommended a curt refusal on his part. After all, were they going to suffer the humiliation of accepting help from a woman, and a seventeen-year-old peasant girl at that? It was pure folly.

But this scornful opinion sufficed to make the opposing clique take the contrary view. Wasn't this heaven-sent help? What could be lost by receiving this young girl? It would be extremely easy to unmask her if she were insane or an intriguer. And besides, if Robert de Baudricourt was sending her, it was certainly because he believed her case deserved serious study.

The king sent for John de Metz and Bertrand de Poulengy. When they were questioned, they answered fully. They praised Joan on every count. To be doubly sure, a commission of outstanding personages, both clerical and lay, was appointed to interrogate Joan. She declared unequivocally that she was sent by heaven for two purposes: to raise the siege of Orleans, and to have the Dauphin anointed and crowned at Rheims.

But Joan insisted that she had to see the Dauphin in person.

Meanwhile, a delegation arrived from Orleans with word that the inhabitants of that city had heard a virgin had come to deliver them. Time was growing short. They wanted to know if there were any truth in the rumor.

After hesitating for two and a half days, the king overcame his habitual vacillation and decided to receive Joan.

JOAN SEES THE KING

During the interval, Joan prayed without ceasing. She was deep in prayer when the king sent word to her to present herself at the castle.

It was March 9, 1429. Flanked by John de Metz and Bertrand de Poulengy, Joan went forth on her mission.

It was night, and the castle was ablaze with light. Lords and ladies in their most elegant costumes filled the royal reception hall. Three hundred knights encircled the throng of courtiers. This was certainly enough to dazzle an ignorant peasant girl who had never before been out of her own village. It could well have made her lose all composure.

Joan was ushered in with great ceremony by the Grand Master, one of the principal personages of the court. First she was led to Count de Clermont, in royal attire and pretending to be the Dauphin.

"That's not the Dauphin!" La Pucelle firmly declared. Then, without a moment's hesitation, she went straight toward Charles, who was hiding in a group of courtiers. Joan made the three bows required by protocol, saying:

"May God give you a good life, noble Prince!"

"I'm not the king!" Charles cried out in vain, pointing to the Count de Clermont. "That's the king!"

"In the name of God," Joan replied, "it's you and no one else! I have come on behalf of the King of heaven. My name is *Jeanne-la-Pucelle.* If you heed the message I bring you, you will regain your kingdom and the English will leave France!"

"And what is this wonderful message?"

"It is that you must put me to work. I shall raise the siege of Orleans, then I shall lead you to Rheims, where you are to be anointed and crowned king."

Although the king was deeply moved by these words, he still harbored mortal doubts as to his legitimacy. He ordered the courtiers to clear the area and congregate in another part of the great hall. Then he said to Joan:

"Now, tell me what God wants you to communicate to me alone!"

Joan then told the Dauphin a secret that she would never afterward reveal to anyone else, despite the countless interrogations to which she was subjected on this point during the Rouen Trial. But we can well imagine she said something like this:

"The Lord told me to tell you that you are the true heir of France, the king's true son!"

These words hit their mark and won Charles' heart.

Going still further, Joan reminded the Prince that he had said a certain prayer one night when he was in great anguish. No one on earth knew what this prayer was. He had said to God:

"O my God, if I have right on my side, in the war that I am waging, come to my aid!"

On another occasion when he had made the same request of God, he had added that if he didn't deserve victory, that at least his life be saved so he could seek refuge in Spain or Scotland.

When the Dauphin heard Joan reveal to him the most intimate secrets of his life, he suddenly flushed like someone who is deeply ashamed or very angry. Everyone in the great hall was following the dialogue at a respectful distance. When they saw the change in the king's facial expression, a few of the courtiers started toward him. But Charles held them back with a gesture, while Joan continued to tell him everything that her Voices had revealed to her about him.

This time Charles was conquered. He could no longer have any doubts. He asked Joan what God wanted him to do.

"Noble Sire," she said, "give me soldiers and arms; have trust, I will know how to make use of them!"

"God's will shall be obeyed!" Such was the king's simple answer. Then, calling his Council to approach, he added aloud:

"This Pucelle has been sent to me by God to help me regain my kingdom. She must be questioned at greater length, and then we will decide what to do."

It was ordered that Joan be given honorable quarters in the castle, and that she be subjected to an examination by theologians.

FIRST EXAMINATION

Joan's ordeals were not yet over. But she would overcome all obstacles. Better still, she would always express herself in such simple, direct language that her words would become legendary. In every circumstance it was her good French common sense that shone through her words, without pretense, pride, or affectation, but also without hesitation or fear.

And so the very next day, March 10, the king presented a nobleman to her, saying:

"This is my cousin, the Duke of Alençon."

"You are most welcome," answered Joan. "The more royal blood there is in one place, the better things will be!"

On the spot, the Duke was won over. He was to remain one of Joan's best friends to the very end. He later gave a deposition at the Rehabilitation proceedings, on May 3, 1456. And he was the one who related the words we have just recorded above. He would also say that he had seen her handle the horse and lance with such dexterity that he was delighted, and offered her a charger.

The Duke of Alencon was present at several of the interrogations of Joan by various prelates and doctors. Joan answered everyone with unflagging assurance. And when he complimented her about it, she said simply that she knew a great deal more than she had told all those learned personages.

However, the substance of her answers was always the same:

"I have been sent by the King of heaven, and I have Voices and a Council that tell me everything I must do."

Thereupon, the king ordered that Joan be examined more thoroughly by a tribunal of theologians to be convened for this purpose at Poitiers. There can be no doubt that Charles followed the advice of the prelates in this matter. Joan's case was of great interest to them. It was so extraordinary. At all costs, they had to settle the dilemma: *God or the devil!* Certainly she was no ordinary young girl. But where did her "Voices" come from? She claimed they were from God, and everything confirmed her words: her modesty, her piety, her integrity, in a word, her whole person.

However, an official verdict was necessary. It would be the same later, much later, in the cases of Lourdes and La Salette, as well as Fatima.

AT POITIERS

The work of the Poitiers Commission of Inquiry was very solemn and thorough. The presiding officer at the hearings was Regnault de Chartres, Archbishop of Rheims and Lord Chancellor of the kingdom, who had been driven from his see by the war and the occupation. We have the names of ten of the judges — six secular ecclesiastics and four religious. All the members of the Commission were known for their theological learning.

The hearings were held at the Hotel de la Rose. Joan was questioned about her Voices, and many objections were raised. She answered every question with a sureness and aptness that amazed the learned doctors.

Even so, they prolonged their questioning for thirteen long days. Joan was filled with holy impatience, for she knew how desperately she was awaited elsewhere. Orleans was almost lost, and its provisions of food were fast dwindling.

To try to hasten the proceedings, Joan kept reminding her interrogators that she had come to liberate Orleans and to have the king anointed and crowned at Rheims.

Some of her answers were so amazingly right that they have come down to us through the centuries as models of practical theological precision.

William Aymeri, one of the judges, proffered this objection:

"If God wants to deliver the people of France, He has no need of armed men."

"In the name of God," Joan-the-Virgin replied, *"the soldiers will fight and God will give the victory!"*

On another occasion, the Dominican friar Séguin asked her, in his disagreeable Limoges accent:

"What language do your 'Voices' speak?"

"A better language than yours!" she answered with a smile.

"Do you believe in God?" the judge continued, for he was a little piqued by her answer.

"Better than you!" came Joan's reply.

It was at this moment that Joan was asked for a "sign," that is to say, a miracle, and she gave the beautiful reply we have cited on page 47, above.

The judges were not content to question her, to examine her both as to her faith and good faith. They also watched her slightest movements, her habits of prayer, her posture in church, in a word, they kept an eagle eye on her behavior night and day. She was even subjected to a physical examination by a jury of noble ladies, who established that she fully deserved to be called *Jeanne-la-Pucelle*, Joan-the-Virgin.

In addition to the judges, many people wanted to come and visit her, see her and talk to her.

One of the most delicate matters in these examinations was the question of her wearing male attire. It was then a scandal for a young girl to dress like a man. However, she had no trouble making two things clear: first, that in view of the mission she had received she had to dress as a man; and second, that she had worn male attire only at the command of her Voices.

She finally won out by promising to have food brought into the starving city of Orleans without opposition by the English, and then to have the siege lifted. These prophecies could readily be verified. They were carefully recorded.

Then the doctors of Poitiers transmitted to the king a long and detailed report, of which we know only the conclusions.

These conclusions were completely favorable to Joan. The tribunal declared that six weeks after her arrival at Chinon the young girl had been examined, scrutinized both publicly and privately by churchmen, military leaders, nobles and commoners. They had discovered in her only goodness, virginity, devotion, integrity, and simplicity.

Consequently, the king could feel confident entrusting soldiers to her so that she might have the means to accomplish her mission as her Voices demanded.

If the king had acted otherwise he would have been resisting the Holy Spirit.

It is a great pity we do not have the record of this memorable inquiry. How well it would have appeared next to the record of the Rouen Trial, whose judges were under heavy political pressures that clouded their judgment and led their consciences astray.

5

Orleans

If Charles VII had refused to act in accordance with the favorable verdict of the Commission of Poitiers, he could not have been blamed too severely. For here was something unheard-of not only in France but in the whole of history. A young girl from the lowest ranks of society elevated to the rank of the highest nobility, taking her place among the great personages of the court, dealing with princes and dukes as equals, and moving with marvelous ease in this role about which she, as a young villager, knew nothing.

Joan was given equipment worthy of a *daughter of God*, that is, of an envoy from heaven. The finest armorers were chosen to outfit her. As to her sword, everyone was surprised to hear that God had provided for it. They had only to send to Sainte-Catherine-de-Fierbois. There they would find an old sword with five little crosses on it, abandoned in the chapel, close to the altar.

Everyone was amazed at such detailed instructions. Her request was honored. At Sainte-Catherine-de-Fierbois, the chaplains knew nothing about the sword. But a search was made near the altar, and it was found among other old and rusty swords. The particular sword she wanted was carefully cleaned and sent to her.

Joan was then at Tours, preparing for her expedition to save Orleans. The king had granted her the title of countess. She was given what was then called a household, that is, an entourage of persons charged with guarding her, obeying her, and honoring her.

A young squire of the royal household was named to head Joan's household. He was John d'Aulon, known for his loyalty and good judgment. He became one of Joan's most faithful supporters, and never left her until her captivity. He was to be so faithful to her that his name would remain inseparable from hers. He has given one of the longest and most complete depositions at the Rehabilitation proceedings. In later years he became seneschal of Beaucaire and was knighted by the king for his services.

John d'Aulon's official title was *"maître d'hôtel de la Pucelle"*—the virgin's steward. Under his command were the two military men who had brought Joan from Vaucouleurs—John de Metz and Bertrand de Poulengy—and the servants under their orders. The page was Louis de Coutes. Finally, an official chaplain, the Augustinian Friar Pâquerel, completed the organization.

Meanwhile, Joan had her banner made, as commanded by her Voices.

THE BANNER

Joan attributed such great importance to her banner that it deserves to be described in detail.

"I loved it," she later said, *"forty times more than my sword!"*

To her mind, her banner was indeed a veritable profession of faith and love.

The execution of the banner was entrusted to the painter Hennes Polnoir. It consisted of a floating piece of fine, strong linen, ending in two points. On one side, and upon precise instructions from Joan, the painter depicted Jesus Christ holding up His right hand to bless, and holding in His left hand a globe surmounted with a cross, the figure of the world redeemed by the Redeemer's blood.

By Christ's side were two angels bowing in adoration, each holding a lily. Toward the tips of the points were the two names so dear to the heart of the holy Pucelle: *Jhesus, Maria.*

On the other side of the banner, near the staff, were the arms of France, supported by two angels, and above, the escutcheon Joan had originally chosen: a white dove on an azure background, with the words: *De par le Roy du ciel* — In the name of the King of heaven. The scene of the Annunciation completed the decoration of the banner. The whole field was dotted with fleurs-de-lis. Sumptuous fringes surrounded the entire banner.

THE CONVERSION OF THE ARMY

All these material preparations were only a beginning. An authentic envoy from God owed it to herself to have more lofty concerns. This soon became evident when large companies of soldiers began to converge on Blois, which was the indicated rallying center. Many of these men were uncouth and hardly civilized. They felt it was a disgrace to serve under a young girl. They had to be convinced by respected leaders who gave the example of trust and obedience.

The soldiers could hardly believe their eyes when they saw La Hire, one of the most renowned military commanders, advance to the front of the troops and say in a thundering voice before everyone present:

"I swear to follow you, Joan, I and my entire company, everywhere you want to lead us!"

But this did not satisfy La Pucelle. The coarse language of the soldiers under her command, as well as their habitual blasphemies and dissolute ways, caused her great suffering. She spoke about this to Friar Pâquerel, her chaplain. Under his orders, the soldiers were assembled, and Friar Pâquerel preached about conversion. Joan openly declared she wanted only Christians who were at peace with God in her army.

"Let no one join us without going to confession: the priests who surround me are here to hear confessions."

And the soldiers listened to her. The moral effect was incalculable. To quote the historian Michelet:

"They had grown young again. They felt very youthful, like Joan, like children.... With her, they were starting a new life."

THE SUMMONS

Up to that moment, Joan had won more moral victories than battles. She had won at Vaucouleurs over the doubts and hesitations of Baudricourt; she had conquered the Dauphin and the court at Chinon; she had defeated the learned doctors at Poitiers; and then she had won the victory at Blois over the soldiers' indiscipline.

She still had to win the military victories she had foretold. But she intended to do everything in a most chivalric manner. With this in mind, she first sent a summons to the enemy.

This summons was in the form of a letter delivered personally by two heralds-at-arms, Guyenne and Ambleville, to the English leaders besieging Orleans.

Here are a few passages from this memorable missive:

✦Jhesus, Maria✦

"King of England, and you, Duke of Belfort, who claim you are Regent of the Kingdom...make satisfaction to the King of heaven. Return to La Pucelle, who has been sent by God, the King of heaven, the keys to all the fine towns you have taken and violated in France. She has come here in the name of God, to reclaim the royal blood. She is ready to make peace at once, if you make satisfaction to her, on condition that you return the land of France and pay for the damage you have done during the time you occupied it.... King of England, if you do not do this, I am the commander-in-chief, and in whatever place I confront your men in France, I will chastise them, whether they want it or not; and if they will not obey, I will have them all killed. I have been sent by God, the King of heaven, body for body, to drive you out of all of France...."

This letter was to be reread to her at the Rouen tribunal on February 22, 1431. She did contest a few expressions which had no doubt been added by the cleric to whom she had dictated it. In particular, she said at the trial that she had intended to say: *Return to the King* and not *Return to La Pucelle.* Nor did she admit she had assumed the title of "commander-in-chief," nor that she had said: *"body for body."*

In any event, the authentic copies of the letter, still in existence, certainly contain the text we have just cited.

THE MARCH ON ORLEANS

Naturally, the English did not obey this summons, which they considered an insult.

So Joan ordered her men to start marching. Her little army left Blois on April 27, 1429. She had sent a large convoy of food on river boats for the besieged people of Orleans, now reduced to famine.

In the afternoon of April 28th, the ramparts of the city came into sight. Joan then realized she had been deliberately given the wrong directions. In obedience to her Voices, she had specified the right bank of the river. But out of human prudence the military leaders under her orders had taken the left bank of the river, without telling her.

Joan strongly reproached Dunois, a well-known military leader who had come from Orleans by boat to welcome her to the city.

"In the name of God," she said to him, "the advice I receive from my Lord is wiser than yours. You thought you were deceiving me, and you deceived yourself. For I am bringing you the best help that has ever come to any city or general. It is the help of the King of heaven!"

At that moment, word came that the barge coming up the river loaded with food supplies had been halted by shallow waters and a strong east wind.

"Be patient!" Joan answered when she learned this. "The whole convoy will enter the city!"

And indeed the wind suddenly fell, and the water in the river began to rise. The barge began to move again.

Contrary to all expectations, and despite prodigious efforts by the enemy to encircle the city, the convoy of food supplies found its way into Orleans.

But the city was built on the right bank. It had no communications with the left bank, by which the French army was approaching, except by one bridge firmly held by the English. So Joan commanded her army to return to Blois, follow the right bank of the river and return to Orleans with a second convoy of food.

Dunois prevailed upon Joan to enter the city of Orleans with him and a reinforcement of 800 men, while the rest of the troops made this long detour.

JOAN ENTERS ORLEANS

Jeanne-la-Pucelle entered Orleans on April 29, at eight o'clock at night. She was riding a white horse and ordered her magnificent banner to be carried before her. To her left rode Dunois, and behind him came knights, captains, and soldiers. The inhabitants were wild with joy, and felt they were already *"désassiegés,"* as they put it—that is to say, delivered from their siege. In those times city streets were not lighted, but thousands of flaming torches lighted Joan's glorious route. The cortege was led to the *Hôtel de l'Annonciade*, the residence of the city treasurer, Jacques Boucher. There, a supper was served. But, as Joan fasted every Friday, she accepted only a little bread dipped in wine mixed with water. She then went to bed, choosing to share the room of the treasurer's ten-year-old daughter, Charlotte.

The next day an eager crowd surrounded the Hotel. Joan got on her horse and rode through the streets so everyone could see her. It was an amazing sight of joy, gratitude, love and respect. People held their hands out to Joan, they wanted to kiss her feet, her clothes. Her horse was almost stopped by the dense throng.

Faithful to her inspirations, Joan thought only of God. She went straight to the Cathedral of the Holy Cross, and prayed fervently. Then she sought out Dunois, the commanding officer at Orleans.

She could not get Dunois to agree to an immediate attack. She had lost her herald Guyenne, whom the English wanted to burn on the spot against all the laws of war, for they claimed he had brought her summons to them and she was nothing but a witch.

Joan therefore decided to dictate a new summons. Dunois later testified that from that moment, an inexplicable and sudden decline occurred in English fighting power.

"Whereas before," he declared, "they were able to put eight hundred to one thousand of ours to flight with only two hundred of theirs, now we needed only four hundred to five hundred armed men to fight against the entire English army."

Joan herself went to the most forward position of the French on the bridge spanning the river. From this position she shouted to the English, thinking her voice would impress them. But the English answered her with filthy language and called her all kinds of loathsome names.

From that instant, they promised to have her burned if she ever fell into their hands. And they were to keep their word when the time came.

The English leader facing Joan on that day was Glasdale.

"The English will be beaten soon," Joan shouted to him. "And they will lift the siege of Orleans. As for you, Glasdale, you won't see it, because you'll die before it happens!"

Joan's prophecy was fulfilled soon afterward when Glasdale drowned in the river, as we shall relate.

THE TROOPS ARRIVE

Meanwhile, Dunois went out to meet the French troops returning to Orleans from Blois. The entire convoy passed under the English forts without being attacked.

On the other hand, word came that the English General Falstaff was rushing an army of reinforcements to the besieging English.

While Dunois' doubts about the authenticity of Joan's mission were probably dispelled, he still hesitated to put implicit and total trust in her in the matter of military decisions.

Joan was lying on her bed, completely dressed, when she was suddenly awakened by her Voices. Falstaff was approaching. Although she had asked to be alerted, no one had come to inform her of the English general's arrival. She rose hastily, and cried out to d'Aulon:

"Ah! Bloody boy, you did not tell me that the blood of France was being spilled!"

Her horse was brought to her. Quickly donning her armor, she mounted and, without a guide, rode directly to the site where the battle was raging in the dark.

At the portals of the city, Joan met some wounded soldiers. The sight of them moved her to tears:

"I have never seen French blood flow without feeling my hair stand on end!"

Joan then threw herself into the battle. The French, heartened by her presence and her vitality, returned to the attack. Fort Saint-Loup, occupied by the English, was taken.

In her victory, Joan's only concern now was to moderate the vengeful spirit of her men. She protected the prisoners and prevented the usual pillaging. The fort that had just been snatched from the enemy was set on fire to prevent its further use. Then Joan led her men to the churches of the city, to thank God for their victory.

Bells rang out on every side. The *Te Deum* was sung in all the sanctuaries.

ANOTHER VICTORY: THE AUGUSTINIANS' FORT

The following day, May 5th, was the feast of the Ascension. Joan decided to celebrate the day with devotion and rest. She went to confession and received Communion. She promulgated a new regulation strictly forbidding the soldiers to resume fighting without going to confession first. She also ordered that the women of ill repute who followed the soldiers everywhere be driven away.

On May 6th, the leaders deliberated without Joan. Dunois came to tell her what they had decided, but hid part of their decisions from her.

"Now, tell me all that you have decided," Joan said to him in a reproachful tone. "Otherwise I won't tell you the secret I am keeping and that is much greater than yours!"

"Don't get angry," Dunois cried out apologetically. "We couldn't tell you everything all at once."

He then submitted the entire plan to her, and she found it satisfactory.

"Let's hope," she added with an arch smile, "you will execute everything as you said you would!"

Actually, the plan was not put into effect and efforts were made in another direction.

On that day, May 6th, the day after the feast of the Ascension, Joan sent the English a final summons, threatening them with their worst defeat if they did not lift the siege at once.

Early that morning she attended Mass, then went out of the city in the direction of the enemy about nine o'clock. She led an army of about 4,000 men. The English, fearing the approaching danger, set fire to the fort of Saint-Jean-le-Blanc, and sought refuge in the fort of the Augustinian friars close to the bridge over the Loire River.

The French, taken off guard, wanted to re-enter the city. They practically dragged Joan with them by force. But she soon returned to the attack, followed by La Hire and the bravest of her troops. The enemy, taken by surprise in his turn, fled. Soon the forbidding fort of the Augustinians was taken and Joan planted her banner high above its walls.

An incredible amount of booty was found in the fort, as well as French prisoners, who were restored to freedom.

Exhausted by her activities, Joan had to make an exception that day to her rule of fasting on Fridays. She ate a more substantial meal than usual.

But as she was finishing her meal, a knight came to tell her on behalf of the leaders that they had decided to wait for additional help from the king. They thought the English were still too strong to be driven out without strong reinforcements. Food supplies were now plentiful. So they needed only to be patient.

But Joan was not being counseled by humans. She turned to the knight and said to him solemnly:

"You have sought your counsel; I also have sought mine. Now, know that the counsel of my Lord will be carried out and will remain firm, while yours will perish."

Then, turning to Pâquerel, who was present and later gave testimony on the matter, she said:

"Tomorrow," she said to him, "you are to rise very early in the morning, at a more suitable time than today, and do the very best you can. You are to remain at my side constantly, as I shall have much work to do on this day. I shall accomplish greater things than ever before. Yes, tomorrow I shall be wounded and blood will spurt from my body at the chest."

She had announced that the French would attack the fort of Les Tourelles, the most formidable of them all, and that they would capture it.

JOAN IS WOUNDED

It was now Saturday, May 7th. Joan had arisen very early, attended Mass, prayed fervently, then donned her armor. A fisherman returning from his night's labors had offered her a shad he had just caught in the river. Jacques Boucher wanted *La Pucelle* to eat it right then and there, before she went forth to battle.

"No," she replied. "Keep it for this evening. I shall bring you a *godon* who will take his share of it, and I shall come back over the bridge after capturing Les Tourelles!"

A *godon* was an Englishman. Perhaps he might be called a "limey" nowadays. She was thus making two prophecies. Her Voices had never been so close or granted her so many supernatural insights. At this moment of her life, we can say that the supernatural flowed in torrents in everything she did or said.

When Joan arrived at the Burgundian gate, she was halted by a guard, but the crowd that was following her begged her to do what God commanded:

"In the name of God," Joan said to the armed burghers who were giving her their support, "I shall do it. Let everyone who loves me follow me!"

Then, going straight to the master-of-the-guard, she said:

"You are an evil man, but willy-nilly, the soldiers will pass and they will be the victors, just like yesterday!"

And she herself commanded the soldiers of the guard to open the gate so they could go forth to battle. When the leaders who had remained inside the city heard this news, they rushed out to have a share in her victory. Dunois, Xaintrailles, and the others were soon by her side.

The sun was just rising when the assault against the fort of Les Tourelles began. The English were defending their position desperately. The French, although performing great feats of valor, couldn't seem to make much headway.

At one o'clock in the afternoon, the attacking forces seemed to waver. The French soldiers were exhausted. Joan grasped a ladder and returned to the attack. The English aimed, for they had recognized her. An arrow pierced her shoulder; she fell from the ladder into the moat. The English gave a loud victory cry, and the French were filled with terror. They quickly picked up Joan and carried her back to safety. Her wound caused her great pain. For the first time, she was afraid and began to weep. Meanwhile Friar Pâquerel, Dunois, and all the leaders gathered around her, uttering words of encouragement. One man offered to *charm* away her wound. When Joan heard this, she was indignant:

"I would prefer to die than to commit a sin. The will of God be done! If anyone knows a remedy for my hurt, let him use it!"

These words reveal her to us as a saint. In that very instant, her Voices came to her rescue, and she suddenly cried out:

"I am greatly consoled!"

Then with a movement of fierce and sublime strength, she pulled out the arrow, still buried in her shoulder. A compress of pure olive oil and lard was applied to the wound. She confessed her sins to her chaplain, amid abundant tears.

THE VICTORY

How was the battle going, in the meantime? The military leaders had converged around the wounded and bloody Joan. As far as they could see, the day was over, and the battle was lost. Dunois gave the order to sound the retreat.

"In the name of God," Joan shouted to him, as if she were suddenly awaking and no longer felt her pain, "I tell you, you will soon be entering Les Tourelles! When you see my banner floating in the direction of the fortress, take up your arms again. The day will be yours! Now, rest a little, drink and eat, get some of your strength back!"

Once again the French leaders were conquered by this undaunted language, and changed their minds. Her commands were obeyed. In a few moments, she asked for her horse. Without dressing her wound, she jumped on her horse, left her banner in the hands of d'Aulon, and went a short distance to a vine growing in the field. She dismounted, knelt on the ground, and prayed fervently for an instant. Prayer was the source of her inexhaustible strength.

Meanwhile, d'Aulon entrusted Joan's banner to the most valiant of his soldiers. Taking up his shield, he returned to the attack.

"Don't take your eyes off my banner!" Such had been Joan's command. A knight who had been following events attentively called to her: "Joan, the tip of the banner is toward the fort!" This is what Joan had been waiting for. She jumped into her saddle, and galloped toward the fort, shouting:

"Forward! Forward! Victory is yours!"

La Pucelle grabbed her banner from the soldier, who was so proud of it he didn't want to let it go. She herself planted it in the embankment beneath the rampart.

"Victory is yours!" she shouted to the French. "Enter!"

And the French, as though carried along by a miraculous force, rushed forward. The English were dumbfounded to see Joan, whom they thought they had killed. Filled with sudden panic, they abandoned the curtains of the bastion. Glasdale, their commander, tried to keep them from fleeing. Joan recognized him and shouted to him to surrender. She told him she had pity on his soul. At this precise moment, the wooden bridge on which the English leader was holding out cracked, and he fell into the river. Dragged down by the weight of his armor, he soon drowned.

In the interim, the Orleans forces attacked from another quarter. By nightfall, the fortress was theirs. When Joan re-entered the city, all the churchbells were ringing to celebrate the unhoped-for victory. The Te Deum, the great hymn of thanksgiving to God, was sung in the churches.

Finally, the heroic Pucelle returned to her quarters, exhausted but happy. Her wound was gently dressed by her hosts. She was unable to eat anything, except for a little wine and water, as was her custom.

THE LIBERATION OF ORLEANS

The English were completely disheartened. To cover the shame of their defeat, their leader Talbot had the idea of fighting a sham battle. He aligned his troops on the plain. In the usage of the time, this was a challenge. The French accepted it. Joan, still suffering from her wound of the previous day, soon rode out on her charger, wearing her coat of mail, without armor.

She, too, lined up her troops facing the English.

But turning to her own men, she said to them quite simply:

"It is God's good pleasure and will that we allow the English to leave, if they want to. Do not attack. But if they assault us, defend yourselves boldly. Don't be afraid, for you will be the victors!"

As it was a Sunday, she commanded that an altar be set up on the battlefield. Her soldiers heard two Masses out in the open air of the plain. The English troops stood motionless, in astounded reverence.

As the second Mass was ending, Joan, still kneeling, asked in what direction the English were facing:

"They are facing toward the town of Meung," was the answer.

"In the name of God," Joan replied, "that means they are leaving. Let them go. It does not please our Lord that we pursue them today. Let us give thanks to God!"

Orleans was liberated. This was the most beautiful day of its history. Ever since then, the valiant city has never failed — except during times of revolution — to celebrate the anniversary of that May 8th, 1429, in honor of the Maid who liberated her.

It was on that day that Joan was first called *La Pucelle d'Orleans* — the Maid of Orleans. Throughout "free" France, as we would say today, the news of the deliverance of Orleans struck like a thunderbolt. There was no longer any doubt as to the divine origin of Joan's mission. Theologians and even an archbishop set to work writing learned treatises about it, and giving Joan high praise.

6

Three Battles:
Jargeau,
Beaugency,
and Patay

HOLY IMPATIENCE

The reader should not lose sight of the fact that all the details given here — and many more that we could add — are drawn from contemporary sources. There are few biographies as well documented as Joan's.

The same testimonies prove she knew her supernatural mission would be of *short duration.* The Duke of Alençon and other witnesses testified that she often said:

"I won't last more than a year."

We should not be surprised, therefore, that she was consumed with a holy impatience to carry out her appointed task.

Orleans had been liberated on May 8th. Joan took very little time for rejoicing and rest. On Friday, May 13th, after a short stay at Blois, she set out for Tours, and the king came to meet her there. Joan approached her sovereign, carrying her precious banner. She uncovered her head and made a deep bow before Charles. For her, Charles was God's representative. It was God who had sent her to him. Therefore he must be God's lieutenant.

The king in turn removed his hat, a rare mark of respect on the part of a monarch, and greeted her. Several witnesses to the scene claimed that in his joy he kissed Joan.

Joan asked for an audience, and this was quickly granted.

Kneeling before Charles, she said:

"Gentle Dauphin, come and receive the royal anointing at Rheims. I am strongly pressed to urge you to go. Do not hesitate, I beg of you. There, you will receive the coronation you deserve."

However, Joan's touching request went unheeded.

OPPOSITION

Even though the French leaders believed in Joan's mission, they hesitated to follow all her inspirations. Their attitude was very much like the one many of us, unfortunately, take in response to God's inspirations. We beat about the bush, we calculate, we measure human concerns against God's calls.

The king's council deemed the march on Rheims to be impracticable. The entire territory to be traversed was in enemy hands. It seemed they would be courting certain disaster if they followed Joan's advice to proceed to crown the king at Rheims. And besides, the royal finances were in such bad shape. It was not possible to improvise a coronation on short notice.

In the end, it was decided to use Joan's prestige in other areas. The positions on the Loire River near Orleans were held by the English. A campaign against the Loire was decided upon, to try to regain these positions.

The Duke of Alençon was named official commander-in-chief of the royal army. La Pucelle, the liberator, would be at his side, to assist him with her heavenly inspirations.

Before the troops departed, Joan was received in the noble duke's home. She was treated with great kindness by her host's mother and wife, to whom she made the following prophecy:

"Have no fear," she said to the worried wife, "I shall send your husband back to you, unharmed!"

The duke and Joan then went to see the king. Joan again insisted that no time be lost:

"Sire, I won't last much more than a year. Therefore, plan to accomplish much work during this year!"

On another occasion, she threw herself at Charles' feet and repeated her request:

"Noble Dauphin, do not hold so many and such long councils, but come as quickly as possible to Rheims, to receive the crown that is rightly yours!"

The king was completely shaken. That was the day when Joan was asked to explain how her Voices spoke to her. She answered:

"When I am grieved that no one believes what I say in the name of God, I withdraw to a quiet place and I pray to the sovereign Master, complaining to Him and asking Him why no one wants to believe me. When my prayer is finished, I hear a voice saying to me: *'Daughter of God, go! go! go! I will be your helper! Go!'* And when I hear that voice resounding in my ears, I feel great joy and wish I could always be in that state!"

After these audiences, the king finally decided to act. First, they would fight the campaign of the Loire, and then they would march on Rheims.

However, in the king's entourage there was undercover opposition to Joan. The head of this opposition was La Trémoille, a greedy and corrupt lord. He was very rich and lent freely to the king at a usurer's rate, in an effort to win the king's favor. As it happened, La Trémoille was with Charles at the time. But the support for Joan was becoming so strong that he had to let the preparations proceed, while lying in wait for the slightest opportunity to move against La Pucelle. That is the way human affairs are, especially in the realm of politics—always prey to hidden jealousies, sordid calculations and secret ambitions.

A CURIOUS LETTER

A letter has come down to us, originally published by Quicherat, written by two young lords, Guy and André de Laval. It is addressed to their mother, telling her how they had the good fortune to see Joan. It is dated June 8, 1429, hence precisely at the time we are describing, and says in part:

"On Monday, we left the king to come to Selles in Berry, four leagues [about ten miles] from Saint-Aignan. And the king had La Pucelle brought before him at Selles. Certain persons said that it was on our behalf, so that we might see her. And the aforementioned maid welcomed my brother and me very kindly. She was completely armed, except for her head, and held her lance in her hand. And after we came to Selles, I went to her quarters to see her. She had wine brought in, and told me she would soon offer me some to drink in Paris. Truly there is something divine in her person, in seeing and hearing her. And she left Selles this past Monday at Vespertime, to go to Romorantin...the Marshal de Boussac and a large number of armed men and townspeople with her. And I saw her mount her horse, all in white armor except her head, and carrying a small axe in her hand. Her mount was a black charger. He stomped restlessly at the door of her dwelling and resisted her efforts to mount him. And then she said: 'Lead him to the cross,' which was in front of the nearby church by the side of the road. And then he stood motionless as though bound, and she was able to mount him.

"Then she turned toward the door of the church and said in her feminine voice: 'You priests and men of the Church, hold processions and pray to God.' And then she went on her way, saying: 'Push on! Push on!' Her folded banner was carried by a graceful page, and she had her little axe in her hand. And one of her brothers, who had come a week before, was leaving with her, likewise armed entirely in white...."

Do not these words bring her to life before our eyes?

Let us take note of the last sentence quoted from this long letter. It mentions that one of Joan's brothers was there, also armed for combat.

This was Peter Darc. His presence is of the greatest interest to us. It gives us an inkling of what had happened at Domremy after Joan's departure. In the first place, Joan's father was probably filled with fear and consternation, her mother must have been crushed, and her brothers and friends must have been furious. But in time, all this had changed. The whole of France was now acclaiming Joan-the-Virgin. Everyone had heard about the deliverance of Orleans, about Joan's exploits, and the king's high regard for her. Joan s brothers now had only one thought, namely, to go and join her, to see her again, to place themselves at her command.

According to the letter just quoted, Peter Darc had arrived at Joan's side about a week earlier, that is, on June 1st. After the liberation of Orleans, it had taken only three weeks for the news to reach Domremy. Without a moment's delay, Peter Darc joined her and became part of her military "household."

Three days later, on June 11th, Joan entered Orleans to rejoin the army. She was received triumphally. That same day she took command of her troops, Alençon at her side. With an army of eight thousand men she moved against Jargeau, held by the English since October 5, 1428.

THE CAPTURE OF JARGEAU

There was some confusion in the initial stages of the battle with the English. But Joan rallied her troops with the cry:

"Be of good courage and high hope!"

The soldiers returned to battle at once, and occupied the outskirts of the town.

News then arrived, as it had come to Orleans earlier, that Falstaff was moving to the rescue of the English. There was no time to lose.

The siege was quickly laid. The Duke of Alençon was to tell about it at the Rehabilitation proceedings. In particular, he related how his life had been saved by a miracle, through Joan's intercession. He was by her side, leading the attack, when she suddenly said to him:

"To one side, fair Duke, and quickly! Otherwise this machine will kill you!"

And she showed him an enemy cannon mounted on the rampart. He hastily obeyed.

Another nobleman, the Lord of Lude, who had not heard Joan's words, moved right into his place. An instant later, the cannon roared and the Lord of Lude's head was blown off.

It was late in the day. The general attack had to be delayed until the morrow.

Very early the next morning, the battle was engaged once more. At the proper moment, La Pucelle gave the signal for the attack.

"Forward, noble Duke, to the attack!" she cried. And as the Duke of Alençon seemed to hesitate, she went on:

"Fair Duke, are you afraid? Don't you know that I promised your wife to bring you back unharmed?"

The next instant, Joan climbed the ladder herself, holding her standard in her hand. An enormous rock fell on her head, which was somewhat protected by her headgear—a light helmet in the form of a skull-cap with neither visor nor gorget, according to Quicherat. Joan fell into the moat. But with unbelievable agility, she immediately rose to her feet and shouted to her troops:

"Friends! Friends! Come on! Come on! Our Lord has doomed the English. At this very moment, they are ours. Courage!"

We can peruse the annals of any nation in the world without finding a more valiant spirit than Joan's.

The Duke of Alençon concluded his deposition at the Rehabilitation proceedings with these words: "The town of Jargeau was taken, and the English fled toward the bridges of the Loire. The French pursued them, and killed more than 1,100 of them."

BEFORE MEUNG

Soon afterward, Joan said to the Duke of Alençon:

"Fair Duke, tomorrow afternoon I want to go and see the people of Meung. Have the troops under arms in good time."

The next day, June 15th, the army set out to attack Meung, held by the English. They met strong resistance, but the city was taken that same day.

CAPTURE OF BEAUGENCY

On Thursday, June 16th, Joan led her troops against Beaugency. Talbot, the English commander, had left a strong garrison there with the order to defend themselves to the death, while he joined forces with Falstaff at Janville.

The siege began with the usual bombardment. Meanwhile, the High Constable of France, the Count of Richemont, arrived with reinforcements. His presence created a delicate problem. Richemont was no longer in the king's favor. The Duke of Alençon had been strictly forbidden to receive him, and said he would retire from the army if Richemont were allowed to come. But the new spirit of the French made itself felt under the influence of the Maid of France. Why these dissensions? Why these rivalries among the French? Does not war demand the practice of a sacred *esprit de corps*? Thanks to her Voices, Joan understood what the politicians of her time had not yet realized.

"Have you forgotten," she asked the Duke, "that last night we learned a large army under Talbot is coming to the help of the English? Did you not exclaim: 'To arms!' when you heard this news? And now you want to retire because Richemont offers to fight under your command. Isn't this rather the time to help each other?"

Moreover, Joan vouched for the king's consent to such a course of action.

The Duke finally yielded.

Meanwhile the English were marching around the town of Beaugency. Seeing no help in sight, the town capitulated.

By midnight, the terms of the capitulation had been settled. The besieged English received permission to take their horses, arms, and baggage with them, in exchange for the payment of one silver mark for each horse. They also swore not to fight again for another ten days.

PATAY

It was now June 19th. This was to be the day of one of Joan's most brilliant triumphs.

Hardly had she won Beaugency than she commanded an attack on the enemy. The army led by Talbot and Falstaff was not far away. When the English learned about the fall of Beaugency, they retreated toward Janville.

The French hesitated to follow and engage them in battle. It was Joan who then decided to attack. Once again she spoke in the name of her Voices and of God:

"Let us march boldly against the enemy," she said to the French leaders who were in council. "They will certainly be defeated. Yes, in the name of God, we must fight them. You say they are fleeing. And you don't have enough horses to pursue them. But even if they were hanging from the clouds, we shall have them, for God has sent us to punish them. Today the noble King of France will win the greatest victory he has yet had. My Voices have told me the English are completely ours."

Joan spoke with such conviction that the decision to go forward was made within the hour.

The French pursued the English, whose retreat was slowed down by their baggage. Realizing the French were pressing hard, the English decided to halt at Patay and engage them in battle.

Talbot took up a position in the rear guard, to contain the French. The rest of the English troops took up their positions.

The French knew nothing of this maneuver. Then La Hire's men startled a stag and it raced into the English rear guard hiding in a ravine.

The English began to shout, thus revealing their presence. La Hire hastily sent word of their whereabouts to the Duke of Alençon.

Joan was delighted to see the Count of Richemont, and said:

"Ah! Fair Constable! I didn't send for you, but since you are here you are most welcome!"

"Joan," Alençon, cried out, "the English are here. What must we do?"

"Do you have spurs?" she replied.

The men answered as a body:

"Why do you ask that? Must we flee?"

"No, no!" Joan shouted. "Go against them without fear. They will be defeated, and you'll lose few of your men. The English will flee and we'll need good spurs to pursue them."

Meanwhile, La Hire made a lightning attack, overtaking the rear guard and taking Talbot captive. Then he fell upon the bulk of the English troops, taking several of their leaders prisoners. At this moment, Falstaff saw the disaster and tried to rush to his vanguard, so it could come to the rescue of the main forces. But when the English saw him move away they thought he was fleeing. They disbanded and dispersed in every direction. When Falstaff saw the rout, he fled at a gallop all the way to Etampes.

Joan and the rest of her troops were just arriving on the battlefield. The English were fleeing in disorder on every side. There was a terrible carnage, two thousand killed and two hundred taken prisoner.

Joan was not intoxicated with her triumph. Her only concern was to bring help to the wounded and to have the last sacraments administered to the dying.

That night the French gathered around her to give thanks to God for this amazing victory.

At the Rehabilitation proceedings of 1456, the Duke of Alençon related that he had said to Talbot, now a prisoner:

"This morning, did you think all this would happen to you?"

"Such are the fortunes of war," was the English general's reply.

In his deposition, the Duke of Alençon repeated over and over that everything that was happening at that time seemed to the French to be a succession of miracles.

7

Toward Rheims— the Coronation

A PICTURE OF JOAN

The Loire campaign had been brilliantly completed. Joan was more eager than ever to go to Rheims. The entire region around Orleans had now been liberated from the English. There was nothing now to stop the march toward the city where the kings of France were traditionally crowned. But she must first get the king to agree to it.

On the morning of June 19, 1429, which was a Sunday, Joan re-entered Orleans, surrounded by the French military leaders. Her recent exploits added to the general enthusiasm.

Everyone looked at her with admiration. A word picture of Joan at this time has come down to us. It was included in a report to the Duke of Milan, written by his representative:

"La Pucelle has great distinction. She has a manly bearing. She speaks little and shows great prudence in her choice of words. Her voice is soft and limpid as a woman's should be. She eats little, and drinks even less wine. She loves beautiful horses, handsome arms. She has the gift of tears, and sometimes weeps abundantly, but as a rule she is smiling. Her capacity for work is incredible. She can remain an entire week under arms, both night and day."

RICHEMONT REJECTED

However, the king, still under the influence of La Trémoille, did not join the victorious Joan to plan the journey to Rheims with her. In expectation of his coming, the Orleanese had bedecked their streets and homes with flags and banners. But all in vain. Joan had to go in person to Sully castle, La Trémoille's property, where the king was staying.

She arrived at Sully on June 21st. Her first act was to request that Richemont be restored to the king's good graces in view of the services he had just rendered. We have already seen how much Joan wanted to establish the most perfect union possible among all Frenchmen. Her efforts were misunderstood. Charles VII, influenced by his current favorite's advice, merely declared that he granted Richemont his forgiveness, but refused to admit him to the coronation under any circumstance. He even went so far as to say that he preferred never to be crowned than to hold the ceremony in the Constable's presence.

When Richemont was informed of this unfortunate state of affairs he left without presenting himself to his king. But out of his great regard for La Pucelle, he continued throughout his life to fight for the cause of France, at a distance.

Joan was deeply grieved by the narrowness of spirit among the king's courtiers. And as she could not hide her sorrow, the king pretended he thought she was exhausted from her military exertions.

"Joan, you must rest," he said kindly. "It is my wish."

When Joan heard these words, she could not hold back her tears. Amid her sobs, she answered:

"Have no fear, Sire. You will reconquer your whole kingdom and you will soon be crowned."

THE DEPARTURE FOR RHEIMS

However, the king had consented to leave Sully to review the troops at Châteauneuf-sur-Loire.

A council was held there to plan a course of action. Troop reinforcements were arriving from all sides — noblemen, burghers bearing arms, and the poor and lowly. Everybody understood that the hour had come to march on Rheims, the coronation city.

The council decided to send summons to the cities still occupied by the English: Bonny, Cosne, La Charité-sur-Loire. And then the journey to Rheims was begun. From Gien, Joan sent invitations to all good Frenchmen to attend the coronation.

On Monday, June 27th, she rode on ahead and joined the troops camping near Sens.

And two days later, on June 29th, Charles VII set out in his turn. He was accompanied by La Trémoille, who was always at his side; by Regnault of Chartres, the Archbishop of Rheims and Chancellor of the Kingdom; as well as Dunois; La Hire; Xaintrailles, and Robert Le Masson.

The French army now had a strength of twelve thousand men. The king's entire escort was brilliantly attired. Now that Joan had won her point, she prayed with all her might for the success of this expedition which she considered decisive.

THE FIRST SUCCESSES

On July 1, 1429, the army camped under the ramparts of Auxerre. Joan was sure the city would be captured without a fight. But La Trémoille was bribed by the inhabitants of the city to conclude a one-sided treaty. The city refused to open its doors to the king but it accepted to sell the necessary food supplies to his army so they might proceed to Rheims. However, the city of Auxerre agreed to follow the example of the neighboring towns of Troyes, Châlons-sur-Marne, and Rheims, and to surrender if they did.

The march resumed on July 3rd. On the way, small and unimportant towns — Saint-Florentin, Brienon, Saint-Phal — surrendered.

From Brienon, the king wrote to the inhabitants of Rheims to announce his imminent arrival. He made an important announcement in this letter. In setting forth the change that had come about in his fortunes, he spoke of the military successes of his army and declared that they had been obtained "more through divine grace than human efforts."

Everyone agreed this was indeed the case.

The king then invited the inhabitants of Rheims to receive him as their legitimate sovereign, without fears about the past, for he would treat them "as good and loyal subjects."

That same day, Joan, who was at Saint-Phal, prepared a similar letter for the inhabitants of Troyes.

AT TROYES

On Tuesday, July 5th, the entire army was beneath the walls of this important town, the capital of Champagne.

Although the garrison tried to resist, it was thrown back into the city. The king sent a summons through his heralds-at-arms, and along with it the letter Joan had written at Saint-Phal.

Joan's message was not well received at Troyes. Indeed, it was cruelly ridiculed. She was just a madwoman, the townspeople said. In any case, she was certainly a braggart. As far as the king was concerned, the people of Troyes declared they were bound by their oath to the Duke of Burgundy. They had promised to admit within their walls only a company of soldiers smaller than their own garrison.

FRIAR RICHARD

In the city of Troyes lived a friar well known for his preaching in Paris, Auxerre, and other places. He had an inquiring mind, and was eager to learn about new things. He was known as Friar Richard. Some sources claim he was a Franciscan cordbearer or friar, but he was in fact an Augustinian. Knowing that La Pucelle was at the doors of the city, he determined to see and speak to her. So he came to the French camp, and advanced toward Joan, casting aspersions of holy water in her direction from afar in case she was bewitched.

But Joan, seeing his amusing pantomime, called out to him jauntily:

"Come forward bravely, good Friar, I won't fly away!"

She soon won the respect and trust of this friar, who became her devoted follower and requested the honor of carrying her standard at Rheims. He immediately set about pleading her cause in the city of Troyes.

DELIBERATIONS

Meanwhile, the royal council was deliberating on the course to follow. Should time be wasted besieging the recalcitrant city? Or should they simply move on? On the other hand, should they turn back and give up all thought of crowning Charles VII King of France? If they had chosen the third course, this would have been, to Joan's mind, a most shameful repudiation of her Voices and of all her hopes.

And yet this third option was the one favored by Regnault de Chartres and the majority of the council. But when advice was sought from one of the king's oldest counselors, Robert Le Masson, Lord of Trèves, he answered very simply:

"My sentiment is that we must send for Joan the Maid, since it is through her that we have come this far."

His voice was heeded.

At this precise moment, Joan, as though informed of what was going on, asked to present her view.

When the council saw her, it was greatly embarrassed. Regnault of Chartres, the chancellor, told her what had been discussed and invited her to express her views to the king.

"Sire," Joan asked her sovereign, "will you believe what I say?"

"I don't know," the king answered. "If you say something reasonable and useful, then I'll gladly believe you."

"Will you believe me?" Joan persisted.

"Yes, depending on what you say."

"Noble Dauphin," she went on, "command your men to lay siege to Troyes, and don't hold any more long councils. In the name of God, before three days have passed I shall lead you into this city by love or by force, and treacherous Burgundy will be caught in its own traps."

"Joan," the chancellor replied, "if we were sure to be there within six days, we would be willing to wait. But I don't know if what you are saying is indeed true."

Joan recollected herself in prayer for a moment, and then turning toward the king she said with an assured voice:

"Cease your doubts. Tomorrow you will be master of the city."

TROYES SURRENDERS

Without losing a moment, Joan ordered preparations for the siege. She put all her men to work. They set up the artillery, they dug entrenchments. Fascines, or bundles of sticks and branches, were brought to fill the moats of the city. Throughout the night the noise of this feverish activity resounded.

The next morning, everything was ready for the attack. But at the very moment Joan was about to order the attack, the doors of the city opened. The bishop and the leading townspeople came out, in the posture of suppliants. They came to beg that the city be spared. They were ready to surrender.

Many things had contributed to this change of heart on the part of Troyes. These included Friar

Richard's arguments, the secret sympathies of the bishop, John Léguisé, and the fears aroused by the preparations for the attack. The soldiers who made up the garrison were the first to surrender.

After the fears the townspeople had just experienced, the king had no intention of imposing severe conditions of surrender for the town. He asked only that Troyes pledge obedience to him. He in turn would grant its people amnesty for the past and allow the Anglo-Burgundians to depart with their arms and supplies.

The news of the treaty was received in Troyes with wild delight. The inhabitants rushed out of the city, and Frenchmen embraced Frenchmen. The next day, the Anglo-Burgundians were ready to decamp. Joan took the wise precaution of standing by as they were leaving, to observe their attitude. She was accompanied by a powerful escort. This proved a sound intuition, for under pretext of leaving with their arms and supplies, the Anglo-Burgundians were trying to take their French prisoners along with them.

In those days, a prisoner was really a piece of property. When Joan saw what was happening, she shouted:

"In the name of God, they won't take them away!"

The king was quickly informed of what was happening. Charles did not hesitate to pay the ransom demanded for the prisoners. Joan was then able to enter the city triumphantly, between rows of her archers. It was only nine o'clock in the morning. And just the night before, the French troops despaired of taking Troyes!

The people of Troyes lost no time urging the city of Rheims to follow their example.

CHÂLONS-SUR-MARNE

From Troyes, the advance of the French army was simply a military parade.

Joan continued to urge the king to have his troops march as quickly as possible toward Rheims. Even from the purely human point of view she was absolutely right. She instinctively felt that the news of her victories was having a powerful impression and practically opening every fortress on their way. There were many such fortresses along the road of march. In those troubled times the whole of France bristled with fortified castles garrisoned with troops.

Joan always rode in the vanguard. Whenever they came to a little town surrounded by ramparts, or a fortified castle, she was the first to summon the garrison commander to surrender to the king:

"Surrender to the King of heaven," she would shout with all her might. "Surrender to your noble King Charles!"

Usually the gates were unlocked, drawbridges were lowered, and the towns would open.

On July 12th, the army reached Bussy-Lestrée. It was there that a delegation sent by the town of Châlons-sur-Marne came to offer the king its voluntary obedience.

Three days later, Charles solemnly entered the city.

JOAN'S FELLOW TOWNSMEN

At Châlons, Joan was given a new and very precious proof of the enthusiasm her fellow-townsmen of Domremy had for her. Her home town wanted her to know how proud it was of the Maid who had been born there and was now being praised by all of France.

Five peasants who had known her since childhood asked to speak with her. She quickly showed them that honors had not turned her head. She went out to meet them and greeted them with affection.

For their part, they were stunned into silence by the respectful homage the whole French army was giving her.

She spoke to them of Domremy. She told them how sad she was to have left her humble and hidden life there, and pointed out that she had left this life only in obedience to her Voices. They were happily surprised to find their little Jeannette was still the same simple, generous, and gentle girl they had known.

One of the peasants, Gérardin d'Epinal, testified at the Rehabilitation proceedings in 1456 that he had dared to talk to her about the dangers of the war, and even asked her if she were not afraid. It was such an unheard-of and indeed miraculous thing for an eighteen-year-old girl to be fighting battles.

"Joan," he asked her, "have you no fear at all in these encounters?"

"No," she said, "the only thing I fear is treachery."

A deep intuition of the future lay hidden in this reply! Joan sensed treachery prowling around her. She had understood that this was her only real danger.

ON THE ROAD TO RHEIMS

On Friday, July 15, 1429, the king's army, led by Joan, got under way for Rheims. By nightfall, it had reached Septsaulx which was only four leagues (about ten miles) from Rheims.

There was a very powerful fortress castle at Septsaulx that belonged to the archbishop of the town. Regnault of Chartres, who had not yet been able to take possession of his see, did the honors for the king and his court. Above all, he had the satisfaction of receiving a delegation from Rheims, bringing the keys of that city to the king, and of setting the conditions that were most acceptable to the king's council.

This made it possible for Regnault to go to Rheims ahead of the army, take up his residence in his archbishopric, and make all necessary preparations for the coronation.

The night of Saturday, July 16th, the whole army moved on to Rheims. All along the way, the people of the hamlets, towns and farms crowded along the path of the royal cortege. Some of them offered flowers to the troops. And the ancient French cry of joy resounded:

"Noël! Noël!"

Everyone wanted to see the young sovereign who was to be crowned king at Rheims. But they were even more eager to see the incomparable Maid at his side. She was the visible sign of God's help to France in its hour of mortal danger. They all understood that "God did not do such wonderful things for every people."

The very fact that Rheims, deep in territory held by the Burgundians, had surrendered—and without a fight—seemed most extraordinary.

The French people were living a dream of glory.

THE CORONATION

It is difficult for those of us who live in the 20th century to imagine what the coronation of the king meant to France at the time of Jeanne-la-Pucelle. She kept repeating that she had been sent only to deliver Orleans and to have the king crowned. For her and her contemporaries, the coronation was God's own seal of approval on the legitimate king, the sacramental confirmation of this legitimacy. Not that the coronation was a sacrament, for there are only seven sacraments, no more and no less. And the anointing of a king is not among them. But the coronation was a "sacramental," in the same class as the blessing of an abbot or an abbess, or the imposition of the cross upon a knight leaving for the Holy Land.

The anointing of kings was a practice known in the Old Testament. But there was no question of it among Christian emperors or among the Merovingian kings until Pepin the Short was crowned at Saint-Denis in 754. His coronation marked the transition from a dying dynasty to a new one. The bishops and the Popes chose to imitate the ceremonies used for biblical kings. But a very important development occurred quite early in the liturgy of coronation. Beginning with Charles the Bald in 869, the ceremony incorporated promises to the nation on the part of the king being crowned. From that time on, the coronation included three essential parts: 1) the *proclamation of the king* in the form of a kind of popular *election*, by acclamation; 2) the *consecration* by anointing with holy oils; 3) the *crowning*, during which all the lords present gave homage to the king and swore fidelity to him.

The entire ceremony was carried out in a framework of liturgical acts calculated to stir the imagination and inspire respect. After the coronation, the king became *"the Anointed of the Lord."* It became a kind of sacrilege to disobey him, and even more to make a criminal attack upon his person.

Traditionally, Rheims was the city of the coronation of kings. It was there, in the ancient basilica of Saint-Remy, that the *Holy Phial* was kept, whose oils were used to anoint kings. According to an account by Hincmar, Archbishop of Rheims, the leading churchman of France in the ninth century, it was claimed by some that the Holy Phial had been brought from heaven by angels, while others insisted it had been brought by a dove for the baptism of Clovis in 496, in answer to the prayer of St. Remy.

The whole monarchical tradition, therefore, tended to make the anointing and crowning the decisive element in the enthronement of a king. And in view of the circumstances in which Charles VII had succeeded his father, this ceremony was infinitely more important than in ordinary cases. It proclaimed his legitimacy, the injustice he had suffered, and the nullity of the Treaty of Troyes that had robbed him of his crown and royal rights in favor of a foreign king.

THE CEREMONY

The coronation Joan had so eagerly awaited took place on Sunday, July 17, 1429.

Very early that morning an escort of high dignitaries of the crown rode to the basilica of Saint-Remy. The abbot of Saint-Remy came forward among them under a canopy, the Holy Phial in his hands. He walked up to Regnault, Archbishop of Chartres, and handed him the Phial.

The ceremony proper began at nine o'clock in the morning. We can have some idea of its solemnity from the fact that it lasted until two o'clock in the afternoon.

The king was surrounded by six bishops, called ecclesiastical peers, and by six noble laymen representing the peers of France. He was invested with the royal insignia as the throng's acclaim filled the majestic cathedral. The Duke of Alençon, the king's cousin and Joan's good friend, gave him his knight's arms.

Then came the consecration in the strict sense of the word. The Archbishop anointed the king, repeating the usual formula each time:

"I consecrate you with this sanctified oil, in the name of the Father and of the Son and of the Holy Spirit."

Charles VII then stood before the assembly in his coronation robes, and a shout of joy echoed through the high vaults of the Rheims cathedral:

"Noël! Noël!"

JOAN AT THE CORONATION

During the ceremony, where was Joan, the real heroine of the occasion?

Later on, at the Rouen Trial, it was held against her that she had occupied such a prominent place at the coronation. On March 17, 1431, she was sternly asked why her banner had been carried in the ceremony in preference to those of other military leaders.

"It had been through the battles," she answered handsomely, "and that's reason enough why it should share in the honors!"

This admirable retort has come down through the centuries to many generations of French children.

So Joan was there with her banner. After the coronation, when all the lords in attendance came to render homage to the king, Joan also prostrated herself, weeping profusely as she did when under great emotion.

"Noble Prince," she said to the king, "the will of God has now been done. For He commanded me to raise the siege of Orleans and bring you here to Rheims to be anointed and crowned, thus proving you are the rightful king to whom the kingdom of France belongs."

She spoke as if she knew her mission was over. It was not that she planned to leave the army. Her Voices had apparently not commanded such a course of action. But she clearly had a premonition that she had reached the peak of her providential work, and her life would now follow a downward curve. She had acted, she had fought, and she had conquered. Now, *she still had to suffer.*

A SWEET CONSOLATION

The day of the coronation brought Joan one of the last joys of her short career. She was reunited with her beloved father. The brave peasant, who had feared so much for his little Jeannette, now heard many miraculous things about her. He had traveled from Domremy to Rheims to see her again. We have already mentioned that Peter, one of his sons, had become a man-at-arms in Joan's "household." Her other brother, John Darc, had also joined her military escort. Both men were raised to the rank of nobles, together with their entire family. After Joan's death they were both adopted by the city of Orleans as honorary citizens. John became Provost of Vaucouleurs, and hence the successor of Robert de Baudricourt.

Joan's father, Jacques Darc, had come to Rheims in the company of Durand Laxart, who certainly deserved to enjoy the sight of such a triumph. They were naturally dazzled by the magnificent attire their humble Jeannette was wearing. When they had last seen her, six months earlier, she had been wearing a shabby red-hooded cape. Joan bowed her head to receive her father's blessing, and asked his forgiveness for having grieved him. The weeping father granted her once again the pardon he had already sent to her through his sons.

Although the royal treasury was in a chronic state of deficit, the king ordered that Jacques Darc receive the sum of 60 francs, which according to present calculations would be equivalent to about 1,220 American dollars.

The king gave the Darc family a far greater honor in admitting them into the French nobility, with a coat of arms bearing the fleur-de-lys of France and the title *Chevaliers du Lys*, or Knights of the Fleur-de-lys.

THE GREATNESS OF JOAN'S MISSION

The time has come to try to give some measure of the greatness of the task accomplished by our heroine, who has become one of the patron saints of France.

Let us cite an English historian.

In the mid-nineteenth century, the English writer Sir Edward S. Creasy published a book entitled: *The Fifteen Decisive Battles of History* (1851). Its subtitle was: "From Marathon to Waterloo."

In this book the author retraces the history of the fifteen battles that have really changed the course of history. He includes the defeat of the Huns at Châlons in 451, of the Arabs at Poitiers in 732, and the Battle of Hastings in 1066 which gave England to the Normans.

And right after these he mentions Joan's victory at Orleans in 1429.

Here is the striking way this Englishman describes Jeanne-la-Pucelle's extraordinary mission:

"It can be affirmed without exaggeration that the future course of every [European] nation is involved in the result of the struggle during which, in the early fifteenth century, the unknowing heroine of France came to the rescue of her country and prevented it from becoming a second Ireland, under the yoke of the conquering English. In fact, rarely did the loss of a nation's independence seem more inevitable than in the case of France when the English completed their siege of Orleans...."

Obviously, he calls Joan "the unknowing heroine" in the sense that she could not know the future, or the depth of the chaos into which France would have sunk without her. But even if she didn't know it, *Someone* knew it, and it is this *Someone* that the French recognize and thank when they honor her.

And here is what a French writer, Gabriel Hanotaux, has to say about Joan's mission:

"Yes, it was truly an event of more than human dimensions that a seventeen-year-old child should emerge from her village and save the kingdom of France from the greatest peril it had ever faced; that she 'lasted' only long enough to succeed and then to grow still more spiritually through the mystery of abandonment and martyrdom; that her appearance and disappearance should have extraordinary consequences and infinite repercussions upon the course of history even to the present time. The times that saw her live, the centuries that followed never stopped trying to explain her...."

8

The
Downward
Curve

FIRST DISILLUSIONMENTS

We have already told how even from the purely human point of view the swift formulation and execution of plans was certainly an element in Joan's success. She changed the course of events by her sudden appearance. After the deliverance of Orleans we can say that the "imponderables" were in favor of the French. Before that, the English had gone from victory to victory. Joan kept them at bay. And she did better than that. She drove them back. She captured the forts on the Loire River. She conquered Patay. She led a triumphal march upon Rheims. Nothing could stop her. She kept urging the king to act quickly. She had the premonition she would "last" only a year. There was not an instant to lose.

The news of La Pucelle's exploits had been like a train of gunpowder, like a fire storm of hope throughout France. The townspeople, the villagers, the peasants, indeed everyone, spoke about her and her Voices. As the French troops advanced, the French cause assumed the aspect of a roaring avalanche.

After the coronation, Joan had only one goal: Paris. For Paris was the political capital, just as Rheims was the religious capital of France. Joan sensed the next step was to march straight toward Paris, to take advantage of the enthusiasm created by the coronation to win over the hesitant, and to restore courage to the hidden friends to be found in large numbers in Paris as well as in all the towns occupied by the enemy.

But this is not what happened. Instead of following Joan's insights, the French leaders kept on as before. They deliberated, they made diplomatic calculations, they became involved in deceptive and secret diplomatic negotiations. Various members of the Royal Council, such as Regnault of Chartres and La Trémoille, were jealous of Joan and never stopped thwarting her plans in the name of political prudence.

PARIS ON THE DEFENSIVE

To really understand what happened next, we must enter the enemy camp for a moment.

The news from the Loire had thrown the English into confusion. The Parisians were becoming restless, and a riot seemed imminent. The Regent, the Duke of Bedford, was then at Corbeil. He hurried back to Paris to restore calm. It has been reliably stated that when he met with his council, soldiers and even nobles wept on hearing the account of events at Orleans, Jargeau, Meung, Beaugency, and Patay. But everyone agreed there was no time to lose in preparing to defend Paris.

The most urgent need, it was felt, was to restore the bonds that united the English to the Duke of Burgundy. By now, their alliance was faltering.

Within the city of Paris itself, the municipal magistrates were replaced by men considered trustworthy. The University of Paris was prevailed upon to exert its influence, because its doctors were infatuated with the English. These learned men went so far as to declare unhesitatingly that Joan could only be a witch spewed up from hell. This was the argument so often presented at the Rouen Trial, where the Parisian doctors were to play a preponderant role.

But the greatest need was to recruit new troops to reinforce the remnants of the defeated armies on the Loire.

Henry de Beaufort, Cardinal of Winchester, had just recruited some crusaders against the Hussites. He did not hesitate to use them against Joan's army.

On Sunday, July 10, the Duke of Burgundy, at the pressing invitation of Bedford, entered Paris. There were hasty and feverish deliberations in his presence. They called to mind the murder of John the Fearless, the Duke's own father, at the Montereau bridge in 1419. The Duke once again swore to avenge his father by fighting his assassins.

And so the ill-fated alliance between the English and the Burgundians was forcefully renewed at the moment of peril.

At all costs, they needed time to find soldiers, to repair the ramparts, and to set up impregnable defenses around Paris. The Duke of Burgundy took charge of this task, by entering into purely formal parleys with Charles VII. He had signed an agreement with Bedford on July 15th. Hardly had the coronation festivities ended when Burgundy's ambassadors presented themselves at Rheims. The talks kept the king of France in that city until Thursday, July 21.

PARIS SURROUNDED

Joan seems nonetheless to have succeeded in getting the king to order the army to march on Paris, but it was to be a slow and tortuous advance.

Successes continued. On the way to Paris, envoys from Laon brought the keys of their city. On July 22, the king touched persons afflicted with scrofula, in accordance with his traditional royal privilege, at the Abbey of Saint-Marcoul. He then turned toward Soissons, by way of Vailly. As the royal cortege advanced, towns continued to surrender:

Crécy-en-Brie, Provins, Coulommiers, among them. It was not until July 29 that they set out again from Soissons. At Château-Thierry, the next town, Joan asked and obtained perpetual exemption from taxes for Greux and Domremy, her native soil.

On August 1, the king set out from Château-Thierry. The rumor then spread that Bedford had come out of Paris and was challenging the French to battle. The latter waited in vain for the enemy at La Mothe-de-Nangis.

It was soon evident that all these delays had given the English regent time to reorganize the defense of Paris. He had recruited men in Normandy. The Cardinal of Winchester's crusaders were there, numbering five thousand. The Duke of Burgundy sent a detachment of Picardians. But he continued his negotiations with the court of Charles VII. He began by offering a fifteen-day truce, and after that promised to deliver Paris over to the king.

It is almost inconceivable that the French should have allowed themselves to be gulled by such promises. But there was much jealousy and underhanded intrigue against Joan in the king's entourage. On no account were they disposed to let her have the glory of liberating Paris, such as she had received at Orleans.

What a windfall for La Trémoille and Regnault of Chartres to win Paris from the Duke of Burgundy without a battle, through diplomatic means!

For Joan, this was the beginning of the downward curve in her fortunes. All her plans were torpedoed. France was repaying its liberator with ingratitude.

It seems that the great Gerson had foreseen this misfortune. Before his death on July 14, 1429, three days before the coronation, he had sent his opinion about Joan. It was this:

"Let the party that is in the right beware of rendering useless, through unbelief or ingratitude, the divine help that has been so miraculously demonstrated."

Being a good theologian, he knew that human passions can render God's graces inoperative.

WASTED MOTION

From then on the opposing armies engaged in camouflage maneuvers. They engaged in marches and countermarches, whose purpose was to challenge each other. But they carefully avoided any direct confrontation, lest their respective fates be decided on the battlefield.

King Charles VII no longer planned to capture Paris by main strength, with the help of Joan's prestige. He probably had only dim hopes that the diplomatic efforts of his treacherous counselors would succeed. But above all, he was anxious to return to Bourges to resume his life of pleasurable inaction.

When Joan learned of his intentions, she spent whole nights weeping. Her one great refuge was prayer.

Meanwhile, in the face of a threat from the enemy, the king's army turned back toward the north, instead of going south against Paris. On August 10, they left Coulommiers and returned to Château-Thierry.

The next day they entered Crépy-en-Valois, where a touching incident occurred.

JOAN TALKS OF DEATH

The French people gave such expressions of fidelity and love for the king and for Joan, that she was deeply moved.

As they passed through Crépy-en-Valois, Joan was riding between Dunois and Regnault of Chartres. Seeing the people's enthusiasm, she said aloud:

"Here are very good people indeed. Never have I seen a people so joyful over the arrival of so noble a king. Ah! I hope I'll be as happy when my last day comes!"

When Regnault heard these words, he quickly asked:

"Joan, where do you think you are going to die?"

"Wherever it pleases God," she answered, "because I don't know the time or place of my death any more than you know yours. Now that our Lord's command to lift the siege of Orleans and have the king crowned has been fulfilled, would that it pleased God my Creator that I could withdraw and lay aside my arms! How happy I would be to return to my father and mother, to serve them and keep their animals, with my sister and brothers who would be so glad to see me again!"

Witnesses to this scene were so deeply moved that they declared in their depositions in later years:

"Joan was a saint and truly came from God!"

She had admitted that only God's grace had saved her from vainglory over the victories and honors that had come her way. But now all temptation to pride was gone. She was too intuitively aware around her of what she dreaded above all else: treachery.

MARCHES AND COUNTERMARCHES

The troops continued their aimless movements to the north of Paris during the month of August, 1429.

Sometimes the two armies pretended they wanted to engage in hand-to-hand combat, as did in fact happen on the banks of the Nonette River, between Senlis and Baron on August 14. However, no battle was waged on that day.

The following day, the great feast of the Assumption, Joan attended a field Mass, and received Communion in the company of her friend the Duke of Alençon and the Count of Clermont.

The troops then marched into battle. But the English were stationed in such a way that it would have required the sacrifice of many French lives to engage them. A few movements were initiated to try to draw the English into battle, but they did not budge.

The entire exercise was completely futile.

Finally, the French army spent the night on the battlefield, and then made as if to retreat in order to provoke the enemy into pursuit. But Bedford simply made an about-turn and returned toward Paris.

Shortly afterward, King Charles VII entered the town of Compiègne, where he and Joan received a delirious welcome. No one dreamed that in that same city the fate of Joan would be decided the following year.

ATTEMPT TO ATTACK PARIS

Joan had not changed her mind. With her good common sense, she clearly saw that the immediate objective should be Paris. There must be a march on the capital. The opportunity must be seized to win the support of the large numbers of Frenchmen faithful to France and to its legitimate King.

But Charles VII was still duped by futile hopes and led on by unsound advice. He obstinately insisted on continuing the negotiations that merely lulled his will to sleep. The two weeks had now elapsed, after which the Duke of Burgundy had promised to deliver Paris. It would have been very difficult for him to carry out his promise, even if he had wanted to, so he simply made new promises.

On August 28th, a new armistice was signed at Compiègne between Philip the Good, the Duke of Burgundy, and King Charles VII. This time the suspension of hostilities between the two sides was to continue until Christmas. After that delay, the Duke promised to participate with his forces in the defense of Paris. But he was very careful not to specify against whom Paris would be defended!

Meanwhile Joan had decided to attempt to attack the capital on her own. One day she said to the Duke of Alençon, on whom she knew she could always rely:

"Gentle Duke, prepare your men and those military leaders under your orders. By my baton, I want to go and have a closer look at Paris than I have ever had before!"

And that same day Alençon set out with Joan, leading a powerful detachment of the royal army.

On the way, Joan had continual proof of the French people's enthusiastic support for her efforts. Beauvais had just surrendered to the king and driven out its bishop, who was none other than the same Pierre Cauchon whom we shall see later presiding over the tribunal that would condemn Joan to death by fire.

On the road to Paris, towns and fortified castles opened their doors in welcome. At Senlis, troops commanded by the Duke of Vendôme were rallied.

On August 25th, Joan's forces entered Saint-Denis, a suburb to the north of Paris.

THE ATTACK

When news came of La Pucelle's arrival with her army, Bedford fled to Normandy, for he realized he was in danger. He left the command to his chancellor, Louis of Luxembourg, who had the leaders renew their oath of fealty to the Anglo-Burgundians and set up artillery on the ramparts of Paris.

Joan, for her part, was making extensive preparations for the attack. But she had to accept the facts of the situation: It would take the entire royal army to take the city of Paris.

Message after message was sent to Charles VII. On August 29th, the king finally consented to leave Compiègne, and came as far as Senlis. Alençon went there to beg him to advance against Paris. He was obliged to repeat his request twice. Finally Charles agreed to come as far as Saint-Denis, where he arrived at suppertime on September 7th.

The interval had been spent in skirmishes. But Joan had determined September 8th would be the date of the decisive attack.

Joan herself led the attacking column, while Alençon kept watch on the gates to prevent the enemy from attacking Joan's forces from the rear.

As was her custom, La Pucelle did not shrink from danger. She led her troops toward the gate of Saint-Honoré, forced the first barrier, and removed the bulwark that protected the gate. Then, standard in hand, she jumped into the moat, crossing it under enemy fire unhindered. But the second moat was filled with water due to a freshet in the Seine River. Halted in her advance, Joan began to sound the depth of the water with the staff of her banner.

At that very moment, an arrow from an enemy crossbow wounded her in the hip. Although seriously hurt and losing blood, she had the courage to stand firm, to have the moat filled with bundles of sticks and branches, and to order her men to attack.

"I'll enter Paris today," she shouted with heroic trust, *"or I'll die here!"*

But La Trémoille was, as always, watching for an opportunity to thwart Joan's plans. He ordered the attack halted and retreat was sounded.

It was now night. The Duke of Alençon had to take Joan by force and return her to the French camp.

A terrible panic had been unleashed in the capital city. Joan kept repeating:

"If you had continued to attack, the city would have been ours."

But it was too late. Once again, treachery had done its work.

9

A
Wasted
Year —
the
Captivity

THE RETURN TO BOURGES

Joan couldn't get anyone to listen to her any more. Charles VII was willing to allow her to retain the highest honors — in appearance only. He could not do otherwise without going against public opinion. But in actuality, he was no longer following her advice.

The day after Joan was wounded during the siege of Paris, she asked the Duke of Alencon to renew the attack against the capital. The troops were just starting forward when the king sent an express order to beat a retreat. Charles used the depletion of the royal treasury as a pretext. He had himself enthroned at Saint-Denis, according to tradition, then set up garrisons in the conquered towns north of the Seine River. He named the Count of Clermont viceroy of the region. Deeply hurt by the king's rejection of her counsel, Joan hung up her armor and a sword taken from a Burgundian. This took place in the abbey of Saint-Denis.

She had broken her sword from Sainte-Catherine-de-Fierbois on the back of a woman of ill repute who had insisted on following the army, despite Joan's strict prohibition.

On September 21, the remainder of the royal army returned to Gien. Charles VII brought Joan back with him almost by force. Then he went to Bourges to take up his residence.

At Bourges, Joan was given lodging in the home of a devout lady named Margaret La Touroulde, the widow of René de Bouligny.

A VALUABLE WITNESS

In 1456, Margaret La Touroulde was summoned to appear before the Rehabilitation tribunal. Her deposition was quite long. She declared she was then sixty-four years old, and thus would have been thirty-seven when Joan stayed at her home in 1429.

Her testimony is most precious, for it reveals Joan to us as she really was, in her everyday behavior. In substance, this is what Margaret said:

"Joan stayed with me about three weeks. She slept, drank, and ate in my home. And almost every night I slept in the same room with her. I never saw anything unseemly about her. She always behaved like an honorable and Catholic woman. She went to confession very often, loved to attend Mass and several times asked me to go with her to Matins. At her request, I went in her company several times.

"One day, someone said to her that the reason she wasn't afraid to attack was because she was sure she would not be wounded. But she answered that she had no more assurance than the other men-at-arms. And another day when she was being interrogated by the clergy, she answered:

" 'There is more in the books of our Lord than in yours!'

"She also related that those who first brought her to the king had thought she was crazy and intended to lock her up in a fort. But when they were on their way they were disposed to do everything she wanted. And even if they had wanted to, they could not have resisted her commands. They admitted they had sometimes had evil thoughts about her, but when they were about to speak to her they felt paralyzed with respect.

"She also said the Duke of Lorraine wanted to see her and asked her to heal him of an infirmity, but that she told him he could not be cured if he didn't reform his evil behavior, and if he did not let his devout wife come and live with him.

"Besides, Joan had a horror of the game of dice.

"She was very simple and ignorant. She knew absolutely nothing, except in matters of war.

"I remember several women came to my home, bringing 'paternosters'—that is to say, chaplets—and medals for her to touch. But Joan just laughed at them and answered: 'Touch them yourselves, they'll be just as good from your touch as from mine!'

"Joan was very generous in almsgiving, and gladly came to the help of the indigent and the poor, for she said she had been sent for the consolation of the poor and the unfortunate....

"In her, all was innocence. But when she was under arms and on horseback, she handled the lance like the best soldier and everyone was astonished at her skill...."

In addition to this testimony, we must consider the witness of her chaplain, Friar John Pâquerel.

PÂQUEREL'S TESTIMONY

Let us now come back to that good man we have already mentioned, Friar John Pâquerel. An Augustinian from the monastery of Bayeux, he had been given to Joan as her chaplain and member of her military "household" from the very start.

He accompanied Joan everywhere and was the constant witness of her spiritual life. His deposition at the Rehabilitation proceedings is dated May 4, 1456.

When Joan arrived at Chinon to see Dauphin Charles, Friar John Pâquerel was a professor of theology at the Augustinian convent at Tours. Those who introduced him to Joan said to her:

"Joan, we are bringing you this good Father. When you know him well, you will love him very much."

Joan had welcomed him with great joy and said she hoped to keep him always by her side. He began his duties as chaplain the very next day by hearing her confession and singing Mass in her presence.

Many of the facts we have recorded in detail in the preceding pages have been attested to by Friar John Pâquerel, especially all that relates to the deliverance of Orleans and the campaign of the Loire, as well as the march on Troyes and Rheims.

We shall now quote only from the portion of his deposition concerning Joan's habits of religious devotion.

"Whenever Joan rode through the countryside and approached fortresses, she always stayed at the home of some honorable lady. And I myself saw her many times on her knees, praying. She petitioned God for the prosperity of the king, and for the fulfillment of the mission God had entrusted to her.

"When the army was campaigning they were sometimes short of food, but Joan never consented to eat food taken by force from the inhabitants of the area.

"As for me, I firmly believe she was sent by God, because she performed only good actions and practiced all the virtues.

"As for the soldiers, even when they were on the side of the English, she had great pity for them. When she saw them dying or seriously wounded, she had them go to confession. She had a great fear of God, and would never have wanted to do anything displeasing to God."

Here Friar Pâquerel called to mind the incident of her wound before the turrets of Orleans, and the offer she had received to "charm" her wound. We know that she answered that this would be a sin and she preferred to die than to offend God with superstitious incantations.

In closing his deposition, Friar Pâquerel added:

"I never cease to be surprised that members of the clergy in such great numbers, like those in the city of Rouen, delivered her up to death, thus daring to attack Joan's life, and kill a poor Christian girl as pure as she, so cruelly and without reason—at least without sufficient reason for the death penalty—when they could have held her as an enemy in a prison or elsewhere. They had even less right to do it inasmuch as they were her mortal enemies. In my view, therefore, they pronounced an unjust sentence...."

It would be easy to cite many more testimonies to the piety, gentleness, charity, and faith of La Pucelle. And it is on the basis of these testimonials that she was beatified and canonized in modern times as a true saint of the Catholic Church.

NEW CAMPAIGN ON THE LOIRE

Charles VII had disbanded the army. He had retained only certain troops to wage war on a small scale here and there. Such military action was insignificant after Joan's recent exploits, and counted for very little to a people who had an "envoy of God" on their side. That is why we say this was *a wasted year*.

We shall quickly run through the events of this period, which culminated in Joan's capture at Compiègne.

The Duke of Alençon was leaving for a campaign in Normandy and wanted to take Joan with him. The Royal Council refused to allow it. Instead, Joan was sent on a second campaign against the Loire, but more to the south.

THE BATTLE OF THE ANGELS

One of the most remarkable events in this campaign was the capture of the fortress of Saint-Pierre-le-Moutier, halfway between Nevers and Moulins-en-Bourbonnais.

After leaving Bourges, Joan arrived at this small fort. She organized the attack and commanded the assault with her usual skill and bravery.

Her faithful d'Aulon was wounded in the leg. As he lay there, he saw the French being repulsed, and then caught a glimpse of Joan nearby, very inadequately guarded. Despite his wound, he asked for a horse and rushed to her rescue.

"What are you doing here all alone?" he shouted as he approached her.

"I'm not alone," she answered, pulling up her visor. "I have still 50,000 of my people and I'll not leave here until the town is taken."

D'Aulon relates that he was dumbfounded to hear her speak like this. Looking around him, he could only see three or four men-at-arms.

He thought she had a whole army of angels at her side.

Suddenly, he heard her shout:

"Everybody! Get the fagots! Get the wattles! Everybody, now! So we can throw a bridge across!"

In a flash Joan's soldiers rushed forward, threw bundles of fagots into the town's moat, mounted the assault and took the fortress. As usual, the town was given over to pillage. Joan demanded respect for the church where the besieged had piled up their most precious possessions.

From Saint-Pierre-le-Moutier, Joan proceeded to Moulins, where she remained two weeks. According to a local tradition, while there she met St. Colette, the reformer of the Poor Clares.

SETBACK AT LA CHARITÉ

From Moulins-sur-Allier, Joan marched on La Charité, a small fort on the Loire River. There she unmasked an adventuress named Catherine de la Rochelle, who claimed she had seen apparitions of a white lady at night. She was just hallucinating, and when Joan wanted to take her along for the attack on La Charité, Catherine would not go. And besides, the attack failed.

After this setback, Joan's prestige declined, especially at court, where so many jealous people were conniving against her. Her advice was heeded less and less. She was kept in isolation, although in public she was still treated with honor. Actually, it was toward the end of the year 1429 that the king granted titles of nobility to her entire family.

That winter, Joan stayed at La Trémoille's castle at Sully-sur-Loire. Her forced inactivity caused her cruel suffering. She had often declared she would not last much more than a year. Now her time was being wasted, and her tremendous energies lay unused.

To quote the historian Henri Martin: "After her return from La Charité, Joan spent four months of anguish.... She felt she carried within her the salvation of a people, that God was impelling her on while men kept her in chains!"

THE DEAD CHILD AT LAGNY

As soon as it was possible to start campaigning again early in March, 1430, Joan seized the first pretext to escape from the splendid chateau of Sully. She got as far as Lagny-sur-Marne, in the direction of Paris.

On her arrival in this village, which is very close to the capital, a group of villagers came to ask for her intercession, as one does of a true saint of God.

She was told that a woman had just given birth to a stillborn child. Disconsolate over this tragedy, the mother prayed with sincere faith that her son be restored to life, if only for the time necessary to baptize him so he could be admitted into heaven.

The child, showing no sign of life and obviously dead, had been taken to the church, and laid at the feet of the statue of the Blessed Virgin Mary.

The young girls of Lagny were praying near the little corpse. Joan was begged to come and join her supplications to theirs. She was far too generous not to accede to this beautiful invitation.

And while she was praying, suddenly the dead child woke up and yawned three times. In great haste, the sacrament of Baptism was administered to him. Then he died again.

Later on, at Rouen, this sort of miracle was held against Joan. She was called upon to tell whether the rumor had not spread that this prodigy had been the result of her prayer. She answered:

"I didn't try to find out!"

Such was the answer of the humble Pucelle, who never took pride in her supernatural privileges.

HER SUFFERINGS FORETOLD

After the celebration of Easter, 1430, Joan continued her campaign near Paris, and entered Melun, which had surrendered to the king. While she was going around the town's moats to restore its defenses, her Voices announced something to her for the first time that filled her with fear.

"Joan," the Voices said, "before the feast of St. John, you will be made prisoner. But take everything calmly. God will help you."

TOWARD COMPIÈGNE

Joan was then leading a small army of about 1,000 horse soldiers. The Burgundian troops were laying siege to the little town of Choisy-au-Bac, on the road between Péronne and Compiègne.

Joan decided to go to the rescue of Choisy. But certain inexplicable maneuvers separated her from her troops. It is not unlikely that this bad management was the result of a scheme against Joan by Regnault of Chartres and the Duke of Vendôme, who had now joined her. Joan was left with a few companies of men-at-arms, making any decisive military action impossible.

Joan thought it best to seek refuge in Compiègne, where she arrived on May 13, 1430.

From that time on, Joan's soul was filled with somber and confused forebodings. On Sunday, May 14th, she went to confession and received Communion at Mass in the church of St. James. After Mass, she stood near a pillar and began to pray. Soon she was weeping bitterly. So deep was she in prayer, she didn't notice the people who had gathered around her. When she raised her head, she saw them, mostly children, perhaps 100 to 120 strong.

Joan then let her tormented heart speak, and revealed the secret of her anguish:

"My children and my dear friends," she said, "know that I have been sold and betrayed! Soon I shall be delivered up to death. And so I beseech you to pray to God for me, for soon I shall no longer have the power to serve the king and the kingdom of France."

Those words were never forgotten by those who heard them that day. Two witnesses were to attest to them sixty-eight years later.

In the following days Joan tried to recruit soldiers, to reconstitute her small army. But she soon learned the Burgundians were preparing to lay siege to Compiègne. Without hesitation she hastened to help the threatened city.

On May 22nd she set her army in motion, and by dawn of the 23rd she entered the town after crossing the enemy lines with her small escort.

Allowing herself very little rest, she met with the governor of the city, William de Flavy, to organize a sortie against their enemies.

It seems certain that this governor was an accomplice of the evil deed that would be perpetrated that very day, May 23, 1430, a disastrous date in the amazing story of La Pucelle.

JOAN TAKEN PRISONER

It was 5:30 in the evening when Joan, leading an enthusiastic contingent from Compiègne, went out of the town. William de Flavy and most of the onlookers thought there were good chances of surprising the enemy in their camp as they prepared for a night's rest.

But the opposite was the case. The Burgundians, under the command of John of Luxembourg, were waiting on horseback to repel the attack from within the city.

Joan, as was her custom, threw herself into the attack, leading the men with her.

"In the name of God," she shouted, *"forward!"*

At that very moment all the church bells of Compiègne began to peal. At the sound of the bells, a powerful detachment of Englishmen came out of their positions and surrounded the French, making retreat impossible.

Joan had neither seen nor heard any of this. She was in the thick of the battle. In her first thrust she had thrown the Burgundians into disorder, but reinforcements arrived to help them break the attack. The men around Joan began to talk of retreating.

"Shut up!" she shouted. "You have practically defeated them now. Think only of attacking them!"

A second attack did in fact push the enemy back. But in spite of all La Pucelle said and did, doubt began to spread among her forces.

They tended to look back over their shoulders, rather than in the direction of the enemy. The retreat began from the rear. Fearing they would be cut off from the city, the French were fleeing as fast as they could toward the doors of the town, and even jostled the guards posted at the gates, thus preventing them from firing on the enemy.

The governor pretended to fear a surprise and ordered the gates closed. There were still some boats on the Oise River to transport the men on foot. Joan now had only five or six men-at-arms on horse-back. Since they could no longer cross back over the drawbridge which had been raised, they rushed against the enemy in the hope of crossing the enemy lines. At that moment, the artillery of Compiègne could and should have supported this action by firing to the death on the enemy to keep them from sur-rounding Joan and her small escort.

But in the face of Joan's peril, the artillery on the ramparts remained silent. Here, too, we have reason to suspect the governor's treachery. Joan continued to fight with energy born of despair, as she found herself surrounded on all sides. Just then, a Burgundian soldier from Picardy, built like Her-cules, grabbed her by the hem of her red surtout embroidered in gold. (This was a long overcoat worn on top of the armor.) Then he pulled with all his might until he had thrown her off her horse.

Enemy archers jumped on her, pinning her to the ground and shouting:

"Surrender, surrender! Pledge your faith to us!"

"I've pledged and given my faith to another than you," she answered, "and I shall be true to him!"

But they soon had her firmly pinioned, and she was their prisoner. Her brother Peter Darc; his steward, John d'Aulon; her chaplain, Friar Pâquerel; and another soldier were made prisoners along with her.

The last phase of Joan's life was opening: this was the hour of supreme trial and the prelude to death.

10

From
Compiègne
to Rouen

ABANDONED

According to the customs of warfare in 15th-century France, a prisoner was a piece of property, whose value depended on his dignity and position. And he belonged to the leader of the group that had effected the capture. In Joan's case, this man was Lionel de Wandonne, but he hastened to turn her over to his superior officer, John of Luxembourg. He in turn could dispose of a prisoner of her eminence only with the permission of the Duke of Burgundy.

Philip the Good was immediately told of the capture, and wanted to see his famous prisoner. No records have been preserved of their meeting, the reason probably being that Joan did not have very complimentary things to tell the Duke about his alliance with the English.

According to tradition, Joan was to be offered for ransom. Now, Charles VII had continued to negotiate with Philip the Good during this period, and it would certainly have been proper for him to try to liberate Joan by offering to pay a large ransom for her release. However, he took no steps to do so. The counselors around him seemed pleased to be rid of someone who, as they saw it, refused to listen to their advice but insisted on "doing everything her own way."

Wasn't she always saying to anyone who would listen that "in God's book there are things that no churchman has ever read, no matter how perfect he is in clerical matters," in other words, in human learning and prudence?

ENGLISH CLAIMS

Although no authorized voice was raised on her behalf on the French side, she was violently claimed as early as May 26th, three days after her capture, by the Vice Inquisitor of France in the name of the University of Paris. This learned doctor accused Joan of being a witch and a heretic, basing the charge on what the English and their "collaborators" said of her after seeing her brilliant exploits. And so the Vice Inquisitor demanded that Joan be delivered to him to be judged for crimes against the Faith.

But this was only the beginning.

John of Luxembourg's first concern was to make sure Joan was put in a prison from which she could not escape. He quite naturally surmised that La Hire, Xaintrailles, and others who had remained faithful to her, would make every effort to deliver her from the hands of her enemies.

Luxembourg therefore had Joan transferred to the fortress castle of Beaulieu-en-Vermandois, a few miles away. John d'Aulon was already there, and received permission to continue to serve her, for he had vowed his life to her service.

ATTEMPTED ESCAPE

As for Joan, her one thought was to regain her freedom. She seized an opportunity to slip through two broken bars on her prison window. She managed to get out of her prison tower, and was about to jump clear when the guard at the castle gate rushed up and stopped her.

John of Luxembourg was immediately informed of the attempted escape. He now had his captive transferred to a more secure place, his own castle of Beaurevoir, which was reputedly impregnable. Three women, all named Joan, lived there: his wife, his aunt, and his daughter-in-law.

The three ladies were won over by Joan's virtue and piety. They wanted only to give her their sympathy in her misfortune. Later on, Joan was to speak of her immense gratitude for their friendship.

Using their influence with John of Luxembourg, these three ladies brought Joan her last earthly consolations. They treated her as an equal, as a beloved companion, not as a prisoner. It has even been said they took her with them to their summer residence.

One matter often came up between them and Joan, leading to heated discussions. It was the fact that she was wearing male attire. They offered to dress Joan as a woman. As they saw it, it was more proper, more in keeping with her character and her lofty religious sentiments. But Joan remained unshakable. She insisted that as a prisoner she was in as great danger as in military camps, and her Voices wanted her to continue wearing the clothing that had always protected her in the past.

What she did not say perhaps was that she still hoped to regain her freedom and return to her warrior's life in the service of France.

This thought obsessed Joan all the more when she heard the people around the castle speak of the siege of Compiègne, and of the besiegers' plan to kill all the town's inhabitants, including the children, in retaliation for its resistance.

How she yearned to go to their rescue!

SECOND ATTEMPT

As was her custom in moments of great perplexity, Joan asked her Voices to advise her:

"For yourself," they answered, "take everything in stride. God will help you, and He will even rescue the people of Compiègne."

"Oh!" Joan cried out. "If God is going to rescue my friends in Compiègne, I want to be there."

"Take everything in stride," the Voices kept repeating, preaching total abandonment to the will of God. "You will not be freed until you have seen the English king."

"Indeed," she said weeping, "I don't want to see him. I would prefer to die than fall into the hands of the English!"

And more than ever she set her mind on finding a way to escape.

Meanwhile, one of the men at the castle tried to trifle with her. Without losing a minute, she fashioned a kind of rope that she attached to one of the bars on her prison window. She slipped through the bars and started to swing herself down this improvised cord. But the rope soon broke, and she fell a distance of over 65 feet.

Soon afterward, a guard on his rounds found her lying unconscious. She was quickly carried into the castle, where she regained consciousness. She sensed she had disobeyed her Voices, or at least acted without consulting them. This grieved her most, and besides, her attempt to escape had failed once more.

In this hour of distress, St. Catherine appeared to Joan. She consoled her, told her to confess her sin and ask God's forgiveness. This Joan did with profound contrition. St. Catherine also announced that Compiègne would be rescued before the feast of St. Martin.

On hearing this news, Joan consented to take some nourishment and was soon healed of the contusions incurred in her fall.

PIERRE CAUCHON PLOTS AGAINST JOAN

Joan didn't know it, but her fate was already being settled. Against her every wish, she would be delivered to the English. The perpetrator of this odious affair was a bishop, who had been driven from his see by Joan's victories. He was none other than Pierre Cauchon, Bishop of Beauvais.

A few words are in order about this major character in our tragic story. He was born in Rheims in 1377, and was certainly a man of attainments. During his student years at the University of Paris, his comrades had elected him *rector*, that is, the representative of their interests and wishes. He had thrown himself into the political struggle, siding with John the Fearless and the Burgundians. When he was banished from Paris for his political views, he sought refuge with the Duke of Burgundy, who named him his delegate at the Council of Constance. He was thus completely involved with the Anglo-Burgundian party, and that is what enabled him to become Bishop of Beauvais toward the end of 1420.

Quite naturally, all true friends of France in his diocese were against him, and this made him rage inwardly.

Cauchon felt the same enmity for Joan-the-Maid as for all who were on the side of the king of France. When he heard she had been made prisoner, he immediately made plans to become the executor of the English vengeance against the brave girl who had inflicted so many defeats on them.

His right to intervene in the matter was as follows: Joan had been captured before Compiègne, but on the left bank of the Oise River. Now, this territory was part of the diocese of Beauvais. Since the action had taken place on territory under his jurisdiction, it was his privilege to express himself in the matter.

In fact, on July 14, 1430, two months after Joan's capture, Bishop Pierre Cauchon presented himself to the Duke of Burgundy, who was still busy with the siege of Compiègne, and transmitted two documents to him:

1. A summons from the University of Paris, demanding that Jeanne-la-Pucelle be delivered to its representatives, to be examined in the manner of an inquisition into her faith and morals. She was to be judged either by the Inquisition, or by himself, the Bishop of Beauvais, inasmuch as she had been captured in territory under his jurisdiction.

2. An offer on the part of the English Government of 10,000 pounds — equivalent to over $200,000 in American money today — in compensation to John of Luxembourg for the possession of his prisoner.

In the event of a refusal, the Duke of Burgundy and John of Luxembourg were threatened with ecclesiastical censures, and measures would be taken by the king of England to demand the return of a captive taken in his states.

THE PRICE OF SHAME

This shameful bargain seems to have encountered no opposition except by the ladies in the entourage of John of Luxembourg, Count of Ligny. They loved Joan and realized too well what was in store for her if she were handed over to the English. But Pierre Cauchon was so insistent that finally John of Luxembourg agreed to his proposal. Being a calculating man, the only condition he set to the bargain was that the sum promised be paid in advance.

In those times, no less than in our own, this was not an easy sum to collect on short notice.

In order to obtain the needed money, the English chose the quickest means. They levied a tax on Normandy, their conquered territory, an extraordinary tax. This is what the king of France could and should have done in the liberated territory, to ransom Joan.

Toward the end of October, Joan's ransom had been collected and paid.

Meanwhile, Joan was under heavy guard. Her attempt to escape from Beaurevoir had aroused grave fears. She was taken to Arras, where she received the gift of twenty-two gold crowns from the people of Tournai, faithful to the French cause. From Arras, after a sojourn of six weeks, she was taken to Drugny, then to the Castle of Crotoy, where the ladies of Abbéville, filled with admiration for her exploits, came to visit her.

It was at Crotoy that a detachment of English soldiers came to take her into custody. She was transferred to the English by Burgundian officers in the name of the Duke of Burgundy and John of Luxembourg.

Winter had set in. The captive was dragged in heavy chains as far as Rouen, and imprisoned in a tower in the castle of Bouvreuil.

Three soldiers of the lowest sort were under orders to keep her under constant guard, night and day.

Joan was entering what we might well call her *passion*.

11

The
Rouen
Trial

PRELIMINARIES

The Rouen Trial was planned, directed, carried out, and dominated by Pierre Cauchon. History will always see him as the man who committed the crime of persecuting a helpless young girl, of treating her as a personal enemy because she had liberated France.

From the start, he had claimed he would subject Joan to an *ecclesiastical trial in matters of faith,* precisely because this would permit him to exercise control over the debates, to choose the tribunal himself, and to dishonor La Pucelle by having her condemned as a witch and a heretic.

He was to devote himself entirely to this one purpose, with all his intellect, his great learning, and his uncommon energy. He wanted this young woman's life, and he would have it. But perhaps even more than Joan's life, he addressed his efforts to destroying her honor. He wanted to drive her to despair by showing her that she had been the plaything of her illusions; he wanted to cast suspicion on her Voices by showing, if possible, she was in opposition to the teaching Church. He wanted to take advantage of her simplicity by entangling her in the artful web of his endless interrogations. This was the infernal plan to which personal hatred had incited this man who really possessed many eminent qualities.

Perhaps never has personal hatred led a man of his rank and character to stray from justice in such a flagrant way. His name has remained an abomination to all good Frenchmen.

MEN OF CONSCIENCE

It would be absolutely false to think that Pierre Cauchon found only accomplices and docile servants around him in the infamous task he had undertaken.

Even among the judges he had carefully selected, there were expressions of sympathy for the defendant. But each time they were harshly called to order. Such was the case, for instance, of John de Châtillon, whom Cauchon boorishly silenced. So, too, with Nicholas de Houppeville, who had the courage to declare the trial was illegal for two reasons: 1) because Cauchon who presided over it was on the side of Joan's enemies; 2) because Joan's case, from the point of view of faith, had already been examined and decided in her favor at Poitiers, by a tribunal presided over by Regnault of Chartres, Archbishop of Rheims and Metropolitan of Beauvais.

This time Cauchon was so infuriated that he had his opponent cast into prison. Nicholas de Houppeville was saved only through the intervention of protectors in high places.

Among those who strongly disapproved of the trial we can mention the learned canonist John Lohier, who would later become the president of the Roman tribunal of the Rota.

As the documents of the trial were submitted to him, Lohier declared they were of no value because the guarantees the Church demanded for defendants were not being observed. Joan was being imprisoned without counsel or help in a secluded place where the judges could not communicate their opinions to her or give her advice. Witnesses of the highest caliber, such as the king of France whose honor was linked to Joan's, were not summoned and the defendant had not been given any lawyer to plead her cause.

Lohier expressed his view in this way:

"They will perhaps be able to cause her embarrassment by questioning her on her Voices. They will be able to win a victory over her, because she will declare she is sure of them. If she would only say: '*It seems to me...*' no man in the world could condemn her. But I am convinced they will proceed against her only with hatred. That's why I don't want to be involved in this business!" And the very next day Lohier left for Rome.

Cauchon's anger was so evident at times and his bad faith so unmistakable that he even interrupted an assistant judge who was trying to explain something to Joan and help her to answer misleading questions, by shouting at him:

"*Shut up, in the name of the devil!*"

This savage interjection gives us the measure of this man and some indication of how his mind worked.

We're not putting words into his mouth. We simply record that he acted and spoke "*in the name of the devil!*"

It must be said that Cauchon's efforts bore their evil fruit, and his work was liberally paid for. It has been estimated that he received emoluments equivalent to over $40,000 in modern American money. All the expenses of the trial were covered by the English regent, the Duke of Bedford, and his uncle, Henry Cardinal de Beaufort, Bishop of Winchester, who was the great-uncle of the young English king, Henry VI.

THE TRIAL BEGINS

The national importance of Joan of Arc's trial cannot be overemphasized. France had not seen anything like it since the trial of the Knights Templars.

To quote the English writer Thomas de Quincey: "Never since the creation of the world has there been a trial like this one, providing it is presented in all the beauty of the defense and all the diabolic horror of the prosecution."

Joan's trial lasted almost five months. Two to three hundred persons were marshalled against her. And they were theologians, canonists, men trained in dialectics and argumentation. She was alone, without a lawyer, without anyone to help, against this throng of dignitaries, of whom three would later be cardinals, and a dozen would become bishops or abbots of large monasteries. She was *alone with her Voices*, whom she constantly consulted and implored, and who kept whispering words of courage, patience, honesty, sincerity, and truth. Yes, Thomas de Quincey was right. Never has such a spectacle been seen in the course of history.

The humble Pucelle, dressed as a man, stood before these eminent churchmen, these doctors of the greatest university in the world at that time, the University of Paris. She looked at her accusers calmly, without fear, without weeping, without searching for her answers, and had a retort to every question. Often her replies were sublime in their common sense, their Christian faith, their wisdom, and aptness.

Pierre Cauchon had carefully picked the members of the tribunal. And the Bishop said to his assistant judges:

"We must serve the King loyally [he was referring to the king of England!], *we must hold a beautiful trial!*"

And he kept his word. He wanted the English to get their money's worth.

He observed all the formalities, as long as they didn't interfere with the attainment of his purpose. He disregarded them brashly whenever they presented an obstacle to his intent.

This was Pierre Cauchon's trial—a beautiful trial, as he called it. The French call it the *Rouen Trial*. Its official name was to be: The Beauvais Trial transferred to Rouen. For Cauchon's first action was to obtain from the Rouen Chapter, whose see was vacant, the permission to exercise his episcopal authority in this trial within a territory not under his jurisdiction.

The permission was granted on December 28, 1430. He hastened to send a delegate to Domremy and neighboring places, in search of witnesses who would testify against Joan. But the delegate failed so completely that the furious Cauchon refused to remunerate him for his labors or defray his traveling expenses. This first, abortive inquiry was never mentioned at the trial. Obviously, it would have been a reason to declare the proceedings invalid.

The trial opened on January 9, 1431, and was to last until May 30th of that year.

THE PRINCIPAL JUDGES

Gabriel Hanotaux has classified Joan's judges into three categories: the *politicians*, the *neutrals*, and the *university scholars*.

The politicians were the most implacable. They were Cauchon's accomplices, his henchmen. A few names should be remembered and nailed to the pillory of history. Perhaps the most despicable of them all was Nicholas Loyseleur, who was the instrument of all the trickery and perfidy against Joan. It was he who went to visit her in prison, his lips running over with false kindness, seeking to win her confidence so he could better betray her. When Joan was finally brought to her execution, he was seen to weep, but his tears could not wipe out his crimes.

Another judge who incites horror was John d'Estivet, the canon of Bayeux, nicknamed *Benedicite*, who carried out the function of general prosecutor, that is, of accuser. He drew up an interminable bill of indictment in which the true facts were odiously distorted and skillfully interwoven with the most heinous calumnies.

This is what Hanotaux says of John d'Estivet:

"He is Pierre Cauchon's right arm, a hired assassin, the user of coarse and filthy language, a man of violent passions. It has been said he died in a gutter."

Nothing better can be said of such men as Nicholas Midy and Maurice Beaupère, both from the University of Paris.

Then, too, there were the prudent and the cowardly, like John Lemaître and the judges who were sympathetic to Joan but too weak to defend her effectively, such as Friar Martin Ladvenu and Friar Ysambart de la Pierre, both Dominicans.

There were usually forty to fifty judges present at every hearing, and sometimes many more.

JOAN'S SUFFERINGS

Throughout the Rouen Trial, Joan was treated in the most shameful manner in her prison. While she was still the prisoner of the Burgundians her captivity had remained relatively honorable and sometimes almost pleasant. But as soon as she fell into the hands of the English, the conditions of her imprisonment became ghastly. Warwick, the commander-in-chief of the English, was a drunkard, devoid of pity and shame. He issued orders and expected them to be carried out to the letter.

For one thing, an iron cage was constructed for Joan, in which she could only stand erect. She was often kept in it. Most of the time, she was held in a keep, that is, the strongest and most secure part of the fortress, in a cell furnished only with a straw mat to which she was tied with heavy iron chains. Three, and then five of the fiercest soldiers, commonly called "manhandlers," were assigned to guard her. They were continually terrifying her with their threats, insults, and blasphemies.

Shame, disgust and horror filled Joan's pure soul, the soul of a virgin consecrated to the Lord.

An all too justified fear of attacks against her chastity forced Joan to continue wearing man's attire, even though the judges were daily throwing this at her as a grievous crime. In the end it was the question of attire that proved to be the supreme argument leading to her conviction and death.

A clear proof of the severity of Joan's sufferings during the five months of her trial was her loss of weight and health. This robust and healthy peasant girl, accustomed to the open air and who had seemed immune to fatigue under the most strenuous conditions of war, was now so extenuated by the abominable prison regime that she fell ill. The English were afraid she would die before the end of the trial. It was then they revealed the fury of their rancor against her. Warwick sent for two of the most famous Parisian physicians, and said the following inhuman and barbarous things to them:

"Joan is sick and I have summoned you to examine her very carefully. *Under no circumstance does the King want her to die a natural death.* He has paid too high a price for her to have that happen! The reason he paid so much money for her is that he *wants her to die by the hand of the executioner and at the stake!*"

The physicians performed the examination and said:

"This patient has a fever. A bloodletting will cure her."

"A bloodletting?" the Count of Warwick replied. "Watch out! Joan is very crafty. She might take advantage of it to kill herself."

Nevertheless, Joan was subjected to a bloodletting, and she showed a slight improvement.

Who can fail to be moved to pity at the thought of this innocent girl, fluttering like a bird caught in a snare, in the hands of her torturers?

Fortunately for her, she still had her Voices. She had never prayed as hard as she did then. She had never been helped, enlightened, encouraged in a more supernatural way by her heavenly protectors.

It is certainly to this superhuman help that we should attribute in great part the beauty of her repartees during her numerous interrogations.

JOAN'S BEAUTIFUL WORDS

We know that all the documents of the Rouen Trial have been preserved. They are contained in Volume One of Quicherat's work, and cover five hundred pages.

Obviously, we cannot relate the entire proceedings in detail. We shall merely cite some of Joan's most beautiful answers in chronological order, as they were given at the trial:

February 22, 1431, during Joan's second appearance in court:

"If you were well informed about me, you would want me to be out of your hands, for I have done nothing except through revelations."

When she was asked if she heard her Voices at that moment, she said:

"If I were out in the forest, I'm sure I would hear them!"

February 24, 1431:

"Be very careful what you say, that is, that you are my judge, for you are assuming a great responsibility and you are pressing me too hard!"

"You say you are my judge. Take care what you do, for I have truly been sent by God, and you are placing yourself in great danger!"

"I believe as firmly as I believe in the Christian faith and that God has redeemed us from the punishment of hell, that this Voice came to me through God's command."

And when she was asked if she were in the state of grace, she gave this famous reply:

"If I'm not, may God restore me to it, and if I am, may He preserve me in it. I would be sadder than anyone to know I am not in God's grace!"

February 27, 1431: It was on this date that she gave the answer, already cited, about St. Michael:

"I saw them [Michael and his angels] with the eyes of my body as well as I see you, and when they went away, I used to cry and I wanted them to take me with them!"

When asked if St. Michael were wearing clothes:

"Do you think God doesn't have clothes for him to wear?"

March 12, 1431: When Joan was questioned in her prison as to whether St. Michael used to remain with her for a long time, she answered:

"They often come among Christians and they are not seen; and I have seen them many times coming among Christians."

March 13, 1431: When asked why she had been chosen in preference to anyone else, she answered:

"It pleased God to accomplish these things through a simple maid in order to rebut the king's enemies."

March 15, 1431: On this date Joan's Voices said to her:

"Take everything in stride, do not worry over your martyrdom: in the end you will come to the kingdom of heaven."

And when the judges told her that her answer was "of great importance" because it suggested she was sure of being saved, contrary to Scripture, she explained:

"I hope to be saved, providing I keep the oath and promise I made to our Lord, and this is that I preserve my virginity of soul and body."

March 17, 1431: When asked if God hated the English, she replied:

"Whether God has love or hatred for the English..., I do not know; but what I do know is that they will all be driven out of France, except those who die there, and God will send victory to the French against the English."

It was on the same day that she said of her banner that had been carried at Rheims:

"It had been through the struggle, and that was reason enough to give it a place of honor!"

March 31, 1431: Asked if she didn't believe she was subject to the Church, that is to say, to our Holy Father the Pope, the Cardinals, Archbishops, Bishops and other prelates of the Church, she answered:

"Yes, our Lord is to be served first!" Joan used this magnificent formula twice afterward.

May 24, 1431: Six days before her execution, a supreme summons was given to Joan to submit to the Church. She answered:

"I told them [i.e., the judges] that all the works I have accomplished and all the things I have said should be sent to Rome to our Holy Father the Pope, in whose hands—and God's—I place myself!"

When asked if she wanted to revoke the things she had done and said that had been reproved, she answered:

"I place myself in the hands of God and of our Holy Father the Pope!"

Such was the admirable young Christian who was condemned by the unjust sentence of Rouen as *a heretic, relapsed heretic, apostate,* and *idolater!*

12

Retraction—
Execution

The Rouen Trial was a prolonged intrigue enmeshing Joan in its tentacles. In the end it became a sordid comedy, involving Joan's alleged retraction.

She remained unshakable with regard to her heavenly Voices. Every effort was made to force her to repudiate them.

In fact, two formulas of abjuration were prepared, one explicit and detailed, the other short and simple.

In order to fool her more completely, the judges wanted her to declare she submitted to the Church, while giving her to understand that the tribunal prosecuting her was indeed the Church.

On the morning of May 26, 1431, Joan was taken to the cemetery of Saint-Ouen, where imposing preparations had been made for a very solemn trial in the presence of the Cardinal of Winchester and all the judges of the tribunal.

As Joan was being taken in a cart to the cemetery, she heard her Voices tell her that she would be betrayed and should be on her guard.

Loyseleur was on the lookout for her arrival. When he saw her, he came up to her like a friend and a trusted confidant and said:

"Joan, believe me. If you want to save yourself, return to your woman's attire and do everything you are commanded to do. Otherwise you will be in danger of death. But if you do everything I suggest, you will get out of this scot-free. No harm will befall you, and on the contrary you will benefit greatly. In fact, you will be returned to the custody of the Church."

To be returned to the Church's custody, no longer to be in the hands of the English, to be out of reach of her jailer's insults! What more could Joan want? She had asked no more than this from the start of the trial, and it had always been refused her, contrary to all justice.

THE SERMON

When everyone had reached the cemetery, the trial began. William Erard gave a speech in which he claimed France should be ashamed of having allowed herself to be gulled by a heretical and schismatic woman. Turning to Joan suddenly, he shouted these words to her:

"I'm talking to you, Joan: you're the one to whom I say: your king is a heretic and a schismatic!"

When Joan heard these words she was startled. Turning inwardly to her Voices, she heard their command:

"Answer!" they said.

And so she answered:

"By my faith, Sir, with all due respect, I dare tell you, and swear, at the cost of my life, that my king is the noblest Christian of all, and that no one loves the Faith and the Gospel more than he. And so he is not what you say he is."

The abashed preacher shouted to Massieu, the bailiff:

"Silence her!"

Then Joan was summoned to submit to the Church. She answered she submitted to the Pope, as we have mentioned in the preceding chapter. Pierre Cauchon declared coldly:

"This answer will not suffice. We cannot bring our Holy Father here from such a distance. The Ordinaries are judges in their respective dioceses. You must therefore abide by our Holy Mother the Church and accept as true whatever the clergy and other competent persons have said and decided regarding your words and actions."

This summons was issued to Joan three times, and three times she declared that she stood fast by what she had said.

Cauchon then announced he would pronounce the sentence. A quiver of fear rippled through the entire gathering.

Master Erard, the preacher, then exhibited the shorter of the two formulas of abjuration that he had prepared. It included the following provisions: Joan would submit to the Church, have her hair cut, never bear arms again, wear only woman's dress, and in return she would be transferred to an ecclesiastical prison.

After reading his formula, Erard added: "This is what you must abjure!"

"What does 'abjure' mean?" Joan asked. "I don't understand this word. I need counsel!"

"Counsel her!" Erard shouted to Massieu.

After a moment's hesitation, Massieu said to her: "If you refuse to accept what has just been read to you, you will be burned. I therefore counsel you to abide by the Church Universal on the question of knowing whether or not you should retract these articles."

"I abide by the Church Universal to know if I must abjure them or not," Joan immediately replied, turning to Erard.

"Joan," said Erard, "we pity you very much indeed. But you must revoke what you have said and do so now, or we shall deliver you up to secular justice."

"I haven't done anything wrong," Joan insisted. "I believe in the twelve articles of our Faith, in the ten commandments of God. I abide by the Court of Rome and I want to pledge my faith to everything the Church teaches."

Then Cauchon began to read his sentence in Latin, as if Joan were resisting. Everyone around Joan, both friends and enemies, counseled her to submit.

"If you consent," Erard whispered to her, "you will get out of prison and regain your freedom!"

So Joan traced a cross of acquiescence on the formula of abjuration.

Just then, a secretary pulled out a second formula of abjuration that he had kept hidden in his sleeve. This one was much more complete and explicit than the first, involving Joan's renunciation of her revelations and the retraction of everything she had said about them during the trial.

By a shameful subterfuge, the secretary made Joan believe she would be simply carrying out a formality in signing the second document. Without giving her a chance to read it, he held her hand as she traced her name on it, and a cross next to it.

Many of the Englishmen present had not been told what was happening, and thought Joan was about to slip through their grasp. There was much murmuring among them, and some even threw stones against the platforms where the judges and the Cardinal were sitting. One of the Cardinal's chaplains called Cauchon a traitor and Joan's accomplice. The Cardinal had to silence him.

Some measure of order was restored.

"She has retracted," Cauchon told the Cardinal. "What must we do with her now?"

"Allow her to do penance," Winchester answered without any change of expression.

"Oh! Men of the Church," Joan exclaimed with great joy, "lead me to your prisons, and take me out of the hands of the English!"

But the imperturbable Cauchon said to the guards:

"Take her back to the place from which you brought her."

WOMAN'S ATTIRE

The whole performance had been a hideous comedy, whose sole purpose was to make Joan repudiate her Voices.

Now, they had only to trap her again and lead her to the stake to be burned.

Joan's first disappointment was to discover that they were taking her back to the same prison. Someone soon came to shave her hair off, which she had been wearing in a pageboy cut. She was also given woman's clothing.

However, Warwick ordered that a bag containing her man's attire be left within her reach, so she could put it on again unbidden. This would suffice to have her declared *a relapsed heretic and an apostate.*

The next day being Sunday, Joan asked to attend Mass, of which she had been deprived for so long. But when she wanted to dress herself, the soldiers emptied out on her mat the bag containing the man's attire. In vain did she refuse, in vain did she remain on her mat to avoid putting on the masculine attire. She was obliged to get up and don the only clothes left for her. When she was fully clothed as a man, Cauchon appeared. He was about to proclaim her action a misdemeanor, when his assistant judge Marguerie said slyly:

"We must first inquire into the motive for which she returned to this attire."

One of the Englishmen angrily raised his battle-axe over Marguerie's head.

It was not possible, however, to inculpate Joan then and there.

Then an unthinkable thing happened. Joan now had no chance to change from the male attire she had refused. The following night she discovered that in order to protect herself from attacks on her woman's dignity she would have to continue wearing male attire, even at the risk of her life. It was no longer safe for her to dress as a woman.

From then on, all her enemies needed to do was to take note of her decision. She was a *relapsed heretic*, she was lost.

On Monday, May 28th, Cauchon returned to Joan's prison.

"Why are you dressed as a man, and who made you do it?" he asked.

"I did it of my own free will and without any constraint. I prefer men's clothing to women's attire."

"But you promised never to wear men's clothes again."

"I didn't intend to swear never to wear men's attire."

"Why are you doing so now?"

"Because it is more suitable for me to dress as a man when I am among men, than to dress as a woman.... I have returned to man's attire because the promise to allow me to go to Mass and to free me from irons has not been kept."

"Didn't you promise never to wear man's attire again? Didn't you abjure?"

"I prefer to die than to be in irons! But if you allow me to go to Mass, remove my irons, give me a less rigorous prison, and a woman companion, I shall cooperate and do what the Church commands of me."

Then Cauchon tried to lead Joan into talking about her Voices. The stratagem worked. He wanted to make her say she had never denied her Voices. If she said that, she would be even more clearly a *relapsed heretic*.

"I did not say nor did I mean to say that I retracted my apparitions," Joan said fearlessly. "Everything I have done, I have done out of fear of fire. I have retracted nothing except what was against the truth.... I prefer to do penance all at once, I prefer to die than to suffer the torture of prison any longer.... I have never done anything against God or the Faith, in spite of everything I have been forced to revoke!.... I didn't understand what was written on the notification of retraction.... I wanted to retract only what it was our Lord's good pleasure for me to retract.... If the judges want me to, I shall return to wearing women's clothes; as for all the rest, I shall do nothing more...."

At this point in the original record of the trial, there is a marginal note stating that for these affirmations Joan would be put to death.

CAUCHON'S GLEE

Pierre Cauchon's machinations had at last won out over the young saint's heroism. We have conclusive testimony about his actions at this decisive hour.

He was seen to leave the dungeon after interrogating Joan. He went up to the Count of Warwick, who was standing with a group of Englishmen waiting to hear what had happened, and said to him with a criminal laugh:

"*Be of good cheer!*" This amounted to saying: "Rejoice! Everything is going well! It's all over for her!"

Cauchon then called the tribunal together, which consisted of forty-five assistant judges. He ordered the reading of the interrogation that had just taken place and also of the second formula of abjuration signed by Joan, namely, the one surreptitiously substituted for the first to which she had agreed.

He then asked the opinion of the judges present. Abbé de Fécamp answered prudently as follows:

"Joan is a relapsed heretic. However, it would be good if the formula that has just been communicated to us were read and explained to Joan, reminding her one last time of God's word.

"Then we shall have to declare her a heretic and turn her over to secular justice, with the request that it deal mercifully with the prisoner."

Almost all of the assistant judges approved this conclusion. To those who were secretly sympathetic to Joan, it seemed to offer her one last chance to escape death. If a formula she had not heard before assenting to it, as was indeed the case, were read to her, then she could be counted on to protest. On the basis of this, the trial would take a new direction.

But Cauchon was wary lest the girl he wanted to send to the scaffold should escape. He therefore made sure the incriminating document was never read to Joan.

As soon as he returned to his residence, he set to work writing the mandamus which set Joan's execution for the next day, May 30, 1431.

FINAL CONSOLATION

Several of the assistant judges pitied the young girl caught in the nets of a complicated and perfidious conviction. Among the most favorably disposed to Joan was Friar Martin Ladvenu, a Dominican from the convent in Rouen. He would appear many years later, in 1456, before the Rehabilitation tribunal. It is through him in particular that we know about Cauchon's insolent glee when he came out of the prison where Joan had made the statements to him that led to her death.

In the 1456 proceedings, Friar Martin is called "the special confessor and director of the aforementioned Johanna during her last days."

Indeed, he requested and obtained permission to hear her confession and prepare her for death.

When Joan realized what was ahead of her, she experienced a moment of terror:

"Alas!" she cried out, "what horrible and cruel treatment will be inflicted on me! Must this body that I have preserved against all defilement be consumed and reduced to ashes this very day? Truly, I would prefer seven times over to be decapitated than burned!"

Then calling to mind what had happened, she said that she should have been put in an ecclesiastical prison, and guarded by men of the Church instead of by her worst enemies.

"I appeal before God, the Supreme Judge, against the great evils and injustices that are being heaped upon me!"

"BISHOP, I DIE THROUGH YOU!"

At that moment Cauchon entered. He was probably coming to spy on his victim's last agony. Or was he hoping perhaps for a sign of weakness in this young girl, a new repudiation of her past?

But if he was motivated by any such evil intention, he was immediately punished by the immortal reprimand that Joan-the-Maid hurled at him.

When she saw Cauchon, she was in tears after her confession to Friar Ladvenu. But she instantly stood erect and dried her tears. Looking straight into the eyes of the unworthy bishop, she spoke words to him that history will never forget:

"Bishop, I die through you!"

Cauchon tried to defend himself, to tell Joan that she should have submitted, and not put on men's clothing again.

"Alas!" she went on. "If you had put me in the prisons of the ecclesiastical tribunal, where I would have found competent and decent guards, what you say would not have happened! That is why *I appeal to God against your sentence!*"

IN HEAVEN

After Cauchon and his retinue had left, Joan turned to one of the assistant judges who had shown pity for her, Pierre Maurice by name, and said to him sadly:

"Master Pierre, where shall I be this evening?"

"Don't you have firm hope in God?" the learned doctor replied.

"Oh yes!" Joan answered. "With the help of God, *I'll be in heaven this evening!*"

Then she told Friar Ladvenu of her intense desire to receive Communion before she died.

But was it permissible to grant Holy Communion to a person who was about to be burned as *a heretic, a relapsed heretic, an apostate,* and *a schismatic?*

Friar Ladvenu rushed over to Massieu who had just read to Joan the writ that summoned her to the Old Market Place, there to be burned, and asked him to go and ask Bishop Cauchon's permission to give Communion to the sentenced woman.

Cauchon quickly called several assistant judges together, and by a decision that openly contradicted his official sentence, he answered:

"Yes, tell Friar Martin that he is to give her Communion and everything she asks!"

Nothing could more clearly reveal his inward sentiments, to wit, that he had convicted and was about to send to the stake an innocent, a saint.

Joan asked to go to confession a second time. Then Holy Communion was brought to her. At the request of Friar Ladvenu, the ceremony was not held in secret but openly and liturgically, with holy candles, torches, a group of churchmen, a procession and the recitation of the prayers for the dying, that is to say, litanies. After each of these invocations, everyone answered:

"Pray for her!"

Intense emotion gripped the entire throng when they saw the great fervor with which Joan received her Creator.

Even Nicholas Loyseleur, who was present, could not hold back his tears.

Loyseleur seems to have been tortured by remorse. For the instant Joan emerged from prison, after this supreme Communion, to proceed to her Calvary, the wretched man rushed up to her and said in a choking voice:

"Forgive me!" That was all he could say.

He had to be protected against the English who were taking Joan away and wanted to lay hands on him.

THE OLD MARKET PLACE

An armed detachment of one hundred twenty men encircled Joan as she went to the Old Market Place, which was to be the site of her execution.

The public square was crowded with people. Joan advanced under the gaze of the throng, which included many who were sympathetic to her and pitied her.

She prayed in whispers and she wept. From time to time, she was heard to say:

"Rouen, Rouen, shall I die here?"

"Rouen, ah Rouen, will you be my last dwelling place?"

More than 10,000 people had gathered to witness this amazing and unprecedented spectacle. The multitude was held in check by eight hundred armed Englishmen. The judges could be seen aligned on platforms. Among them was the Cardinal of Winchester, flanked by two of his bishops.

On a masonry base that had been erected for the purpose, an enormous pyre had been raised, allowing the victim to be seen by everyone. Facing the stake, a large sign had been set up on a high post, listing all the crimes of which Joan had been convicted.

Nicholas Midy, a doctor from Paris, was designated to give the sermon. He closed with the traditional words:

"Joan, go in peace! The Church can no longer defend you, and so she leaves you to the secular arm."

Cauchon then read the sentence of conviction and mentioned the reasons on which, according to the tribunal, it was based. Then, in his turn, he surrendered the convicted girl to the secular arm.

According to law, the civil tribunal should have taken her into custody at once and also pronounced a regular sentence on her before proceeding to the execution, for this was not mentioned in the ecclesiastical conviction. But the English were in far too great a hurry to be rid of her to observe the regular procedures.

Joan fell to her knees, and in a loud, clear voice said fervent prayers to the Blessed Trinity, to the Blessed Virgin Mary, to the saints of heaven, and in particular to her Voices. She made an act of faith, protesting that she was not and would never be a heretic. Finally, she asked her king's forgiveness. One of her last thoughts was of him. For her, Charles VII was France.

It was such a moving sight. Joan's prayers were so noble and beautiful that everyone around her was sobbing, even the English.

Indeed, when she asked that a cross be given her to mount to the stake, it was an English soldier who made one from two pieces of wood and put it into her hands. Joan kissed it devoutly. Then she asked to have a crucifix before her during her execution. Massieu ran through the crowd to the neighboring church of the Holy Savior, and brought back a processional cross. He held it up for her to kiss, and kept it before her eyes to the end.

DEATH BY FIRE

Several Englishmen felt that these scenes had lasted long enough. Several of them came up to the platform and shouted to Massieu:

"Hey there, priest! Are you going to keep us here for dinner?"

So Joan was led to the funeral pyre. The civil judge said only these words:

"Take her away!" He refused to pass any sentence.

Warwick shouted to the executioner:

"Do your duty!"

Two sergeants seized Joan, made her go up the steps of the funeral pyre, and tied her to the post. A mitre was put on her head, bearing the words we have already mentioned:

Heretic, relapsed heretic, apostate, idolater.

The two friars, Ladvenu and Ysambart de la Pierre, stayed with her to the end.

Joan said to them:

"I beg of you, when the fire is kindled, hold the crucifix before my eyes, and keep showing it to me. I declare to you once more: my Voices were from God. It is by divine command that I did everything good that I did. No, no, my Voices did not deceive me! They really came from heaven!"

Meanwhile, the executioner had set the stake on fire, and a heavy smoke was beginning to rise.

"There's the fire!" Joan cried out to the two friars. "Go down quickly, but hold the cross up before my eyes to the very last instant!"

She wanted to die "with Christ, in Christ."

The smoke continued to grow denser, and flames spurted up from all sides around Joan.

From the midst of the flames, Joan was heard to cry out several times:

"Jesus!"

An English soldier had sworn to throw some wood on the fire. He approached, picked up some vine branches, and brought them to the stake. At that very moment, the dying Joan uttered a great cry, her last:

"Jesus!"

At the word, the Englishman fell in a faint.

ASHES IN THE SEINE

Very few of the witnesses to this sight, so reminiscent of Golgotha, could hold back their tears. Neither Cauchon, nor Winchester, any more than Loyseleur, could control their emotions. But their hatred prevailed. Winchester ordered that the victim's ashes be collected and thrown into the Seine, so they could not become relics to be honored by the faithful.

The troops were ordered to march past the stake where the work of destruction was almost finished. The executioner, whose name was Thirache, stirred the ashes to find Joan's remains. But to his amazement he found La Pucelle's heart untouched by the flames and still bleeding. He therefore re-kindled the flames, threw some oil, sulphur, and coal on them, to consume this heart. But when he returned to collect Joan's ashes, thinking her heart was now burned up, he found it again intact and humid with blood.

When his baneful work was finally completed, the terrified executioner fled to the convent of the Dominican friars, and shouted to Friars Ladvenu and Ysambart de la Pierre:

"God will never forgive me! I've burned a saint!"

And he confessed his sin then and there.

But Winchester's order had to be carried out. Joan's remains were therefore shoveled into a sack, together with her heart. That evening, around five o'clock, the sack was thrown into the river at the Mathilde bridge. Such was the fate of the virgin's charred body.

A SAINT!

Almost immediately, sorrow and regret found expression among both the English and the French who had witnessed Joan's glorious end.

The executioner was not alone in proclaiming he had burned a saint. Almost as one, the entire throng was of the same mind.

Canon John Alespée, of the chapter of Rouen, cried out:

"Would to God my soul were where I think the soul of this young girl is!" And he wept profusely as he spoke.

John Tressart, the official secretary to the English King, Henry VI, said after the execution:

"A faithful Christian woman has just died. I believe her soul is in the hands of God, and I believe all who have approved of her conviction are damned!"

Later on, he said something else to Pierre Cusquel that history has remembered. His words have been recorded in Cusquel's deposition at the Rehabilitation proceedings, on May 12, 1456:

"I had not wanted to be present at Joan's execution because I could not have stood it. But it was the general opinion that a great injustice had been done to Joan. And I heard Master John Tressart, secretary to the King of England, say to me, right after he came back from the execution and weeping over everything he had just seen: *'We are all lost, because a saint has just been burned to death!'* And he told me that even in the midst of the flames she never stopped crying out the name of Jesus."

13

Rehabilitation—
Glorification

PROPHECIES FULFILLED

Joan made many prophecies announcing the defeat of the English and their expulsion from France. She likewise said that her judges should tremble for having passed sentence against her.

Authentic history proves that the facts have corroborated her words.

Nicholas Midy, the preacher at the Old Market Place, was stricken with leprosy. Cauchon, who had to accept the bishopric of Lisieux instead of Rouen, was excommunicated by the Council of Basle for refusing to pay the sums of money he owed to the Roman Curia. He died suddenly on December 18, 1442. Loyseleur, the traitor, died a poor man from a stroke of apoplexy. He was found lying in a muddy ditch.

By 1435, Philip the Good, Duke of Burgundy, signed a treaty of peace with Charles VII. The Duke of Bedford, Regent of France, was so distressed by this that it has been said he died of discouragement while still young, on September 14, 1435. His death occurred in the same castle of Bouvreuil where Joan had once been imprisoned.

The Count of Warwick also died prematurely in the same castle.

The prosecutor Estivet met a shameful death.

The power of the English continued to dwindle in France. Joan had clearly predicted: "Before seven years have passed the English will lose a greater wager than the one they lost before Orleans." That amounted to saying they would lose all their holdings in France.

This prediction was fullfilled six years later, in 1437, when Paris was recaptured by the French.

La Trémoille, Joan's great adversary, lost the king's favor. Richemont, his rival, was restored to prominence. It was he who recaptured Paris and drove the English out, and with them Pierre Cauchon who must have remembered La Pucelle's prophecy.

The city of Rouen was not retaken until 1449. The victories of Formigny in 1450, and Castillon on July 17, 1453, brought back to France the beautiful provinces of Normandy and Guyenne. Thus ended the Hundred Years' War.

The kingdom of France was indeed liberated. And Charles VII had an obligation to restore to honor the young girl who had sacrificed herself for him and whom the English had sought to vilify.

THE REHABILITATION PROCEEDINGS

The king of France found support from the most eminent men in France in his efforts to rehabilitate Joan-the-Maid's honor.

Cardinal d'Estouteville, Archbishop of Rouen and one of the most outstanding personages of his time, took charge of initiating the Rehabilitation proceedings in 1452. He was helped in this work by John Bréhal, Inquisitor of France.

At the king's command, John Bréhal went to Rome, bearing a petition from Isabelle Romée, Joan's mother, and from Peter and John, Joan's two brothers.

Pope Callixtus III (a member of the Borgia family) published a rescript ordering a revision of the trial. Joan's story was well known in Rome. In fact, Cardinal Piccolomini, who was to succeed Callixtus III as Pope soon afterward, had written things about her of great historic value.

The tribunal for the reexamination was presided over by John Juvenal des Ursins, Archbishop of Rheims. Its judges also included such eminent men as William Chartier, Bishop of Paris, and Richard de Longueil, Bishop of Coutances.

Long and meticulous inquiries were made.

Throughout our account, we have cited many depositions in connection with the Rehabilitation proceedings, at Domremy, Vaucouleurs, Rouen, Orleans, Paris, and other places.

The Rehabilitation proceedings lasted eight months, three months longer than the original Rouen Trial which condemned Joan. Quicherat has published the entire proceedings, and they have been preserved.

The final sentence annulled the one of 1431. It declared the twelve articles retained against Joan of Arc to be calumnious; the abjuration at the cemetery of Saint-Ouen totally null and void by law, inasmuch as it was wrested by force, out of fear of the executioner, through threats of fire, and without the defendant's knowing what she was being made to sign, or even understanding the terms used in the document.

The two trials for "heresy" and "relapse into heresy" were thus devoid of value, tainted by deceit, fraud, calumny, and injustice, and filled with contradictions and errors of fact and law.

Once the sentence of 1431 was annulled, the Rehabilitation tribunal of 1456 declared that Joan and her family were cleared of any stain of infamy. It ordered a double ceremony of public reparation, one at the cemetery of Saint-Ouen, and the other at the Old Market Place in Rouen.

POSTERITY

Joan's contemporaries wrote extensively about her. Later on, writers adopted various positions in evaluating her. It was not until the eighteenth century that serious historical studies began to appear about

La Pucelle. The historian Lenglet-Dufresnoy carefully studied the two sets of proceedings, whose
minutes had been preserved, and he was conquered.

The nineteenth century was still more favorable to Joan's memory. Chateaubriand wrote the
following passage, in discussing the Hundred Years'
War:

"In misfortune as well as in prosperity, there
was an element of the miraculous in the history of
those times. An extraordinary vision had driven
Charles VI out of his mind; mysterious revelations
strengthened La Pucelle's arm; the kingdom of
France was snatched from the lineage of St. Louis
by a supernatural cause; it was restored to his posterity by a miracle. In Joan's character we find the
naiveté of the peasant, the weakness of woman, the
inspiration of the saint, and the courage of a heroine...."

Thus, this great writer made reparation for
the insults Voltaire had heaped upon Joan.

After Quicherat's great work of publishing
source materials on Joan of Arc, which we have used
throughout the present book, many predominate.
First, the trend to give a simple account of the facts,
accepting the supernatural, which, as we have said,
is everywhere at work in Joan's story. Then there was
the rationalistic trend, which sought explanations,
that most often proved to be either superficial or contrary to the most assured truths. To quote Gabriel
Hanotaux: "Rationalism is self-sufficient, and brings
all problems within its own compass."

This is the time to repeat what Joan of Arc
said so well: "There are more things in God's books
than in the books of scholars!"

It is no exaggeration to say that all great historians, painters and sculptors have striven to repro-
duce Joan of Arc. That is what everyone has come to
call her. And yet she herself always preferred the
name of *Jeanne-la-Pucelle*, that is, Joan-the-Virgin
or Joan-the-Maid.

THE HALO OF THE SAINTS

Those who stood near the stake at Rouen said: "We have burned a saint!" Public piety and admiration canonized Joan many times over. But only the supreme authority of the Church could pronounce irrevocable decisions on this subject.

The Church takes a long time to make such decisions, which are based on prolonged and careful inquiries into the life of the candidate, to ascertain if he or she practiced the Christian virtues to a heroic degree. In addition, God's own mark of approval is sought. To this end, the promoters of the prospective saint's cause are asked to vouch for *four authentic miracles* obtained after the death of the candidate for sainthood, to secure his or her beatification, and *two more*, obtained after the beatification to proceed to the canonization.

However, it is customary for the Holy Father to dispense with one of the miracles required for beatification if the candidate has founded a religious order or congregation.

In Joan's case, this dispensation was granted because she had saved France. Thus, *three miracles* sufficed for her beatification.

TOWARD BEATIFICATION

It was Bishop Dupanloup of Orleans who initiated the first request in 1869 for the introduction of Joan of Arc's cause, when Pius IX was Pope. This honor rightly belonged to the bishop of the city that had never forgotten its liberation and celebrated its memory yearly with civil and religious ceremonies.

All the bishops of France supported Bishop Dupanloup's petition, as well as a large number of prelates from other lands. Then the preparatory inquiries began.

It was a great Pope, Leo XIII, who ordered a favorable conclusion to the proceedings, by declaring on January 24, 1894, that there was just cause to seek her beatification.

And he added with emotion:

"Joan is ours!"

The cause followed its prescribed course. The best known and most highly respected historians were convoked. They came and made depositions of what they knew about Joan and what they thought of her, not only from the human or patriotic point of view, but also from the vantage point of Christianity.

Following Leo XIII, Pius X, who was to be canonized in later years, took Joan's cause to heart. As he expressed it, "Joan had shone like a new star destined to be the glory not only of France but of the Universal Church as well."

On January 6, 1904, Pius X issued the most important decree among those that prepare the way for a beatification, namely, the decree as to the candidate's *heroic virtue.*

THE THREE MIRACLES

The time had come to officially establish the three miracles necessary for Joan's beatification.

Among the many favors attributed to Joan, three cures were chosen, deemed to be miraculous after long and rigorous investigations. In 1897, Sister Thérèse of St. Augustine had been cured of an ulcer at Orleans. Sister Julie Gauthier was cured of a cancerous ulcer at Faverolles, near Evreux. Sister Marie Sagnier of the Congregation of the Holy Family was also miraculously cured at Frages, in the diocese of Arras.

These miracles were accepted as authentic.

The minutes of this twofold inquiry were published in two imposing volumes in Rome. The first, dealing with Joan's virtues, was published in 1901. The second, concerning the miracles, was published in 1907.

On December 13, 1908, Pope Pius X solemnly published the decree that accepted these three miracles as authentic.

And so the long-awaited beatification finally took place in a solemn ceremony in St. Peter's Basilica at Rome, April 18, 1909.

We should note that Joan's beatification did not honor her solely in her heroic death, as might have been thought if she had been beatified as a "martyr," the way some would have preferred.

Contrary to what has been said by certain writers who are completely ignorant of the theological aspects of the matter, it was a far greater honor for Joan to be proclaimed a "virgin," and "blessed," and then a "saint." This amounted to granting the honor of sainthood to her whole earthly life and not merely to her death.

Besides, we should remember that "it is not *the suffering* but *the cause* that makes a martyr." This means that to be declared a martyr it is not enough to have died in a tragic manner and with the courage of a hero. One must also have given one's life "for the Faith," that is to say, to have been put to death "out of hatred for the Faith." Now, while the English and the judges who had sold themselves to their cause had political reasons for convicting and executing Joan of Arc, it would be difficult to prove that they burned her to death at Rouen "out of hatred for the Christian Faith."

THE CANONIZATION

The beatification ceremonies had scarcely been celebrated in all the parishes of France when the eloquent and active Bishop Touchet of Orleans began storming heaven for the two miracles needed for Joan's canonization.

These two miracles were obtained and authenticated without too much delay. The canonization would have followed soon afterward except for World

War I, which put a stop to all such activities from 1914 to 1918.

Finally, soon after that war, Pope Benedict XV proceeded to canonize Joan on May 9, 1920.

The liturgical feast of St. Joan of Arc was set on May 30, the date of her death. In France, a law passed on July 10, 1920, and voted for unanimously by the country's elected representatives, proclaimed as a national holiday the anniversary of the deliverance of Orleans by Joan, on May 8th.

TWO PERSONAL MEMORIES

As I complete this little book, I take the liberty of mentioning two personal memories which redound to the glory of St. Joan of Arc.

The first concerns one of the two miracles accepted for the canonization. It was my honor to be chosen by Bishop Touchet to be the official reporter of this miracle, which took place at Lourdes, and of which I was one of many witnesses.

This was the case of a young invalid from Lyons, France, named Thérèse Bellin. I have given from my personal notes, taken the very day of the miracle, a detailed account of everything that happened. This account was published in the periodical *Ecclesia*, in its May, 1953 issue.

The date was August 22, 1909. Bishop Touchet happened to be at Lourdes with a pilgrimage from his diocese. He asked permission to offer the usual invocations during the procession of the Blessed Sacrament that afternoon, and to add *just once* during the ceremony three invocations to Joan of Arc. His intention was to obtain a miracle to support the cause of her canonization.

Thérèse Bellin lay unconscious among the sick lined up on the esplanade. She remained unconscious when the Blessed Sacrament passed before her. But at the first invocation to Blessed Joan of Arc she opened her eyes; at the second, she sat up on her stretcher: and at the third invocation, she felt she had been cured. I saw her a few moments later. I then informed Bishop Touchet of the miraculous cure. As he had to leave Lourdes, he asked me to give him a complete report on this cure.

I questioned at great length the young woman who had been miraculously cured, as well as her godmother who had accompanied her. They told me the various stages of her sickness, the names of the physicians who had been treating her, the operations she had had, the remedies that had been used without effect, and finally about the cure.

This was carefully checked and rechecked by competent authorities, and the miracle was registered as authentic.

Here is another of my memories. The same Bishop Touchet of Orleans told me that before the beatification he had sent for a famous Belgian historian to come and make a deposition on Joan at Orleans. This historian, Godfrey Kurth, was very well known for his scientific works and the high caliber of his erudition and philosophy of history.

When Dr. Kurth had finished giving his deposition, the Bishop of Orleans, who was presiding over the tribunal, asked the historian to give his general impression of Joan of Arc.

"Then," the bishop told me, "Godfrey Kurth stood up straight and tall and made the following declaration in solemn tones:

"'Your Excellency, I have been teaching history for forty years. I cannot claim that I know history, for no one knows history. But what I can say is that, in all my research, leaving aside our Sacred Books and the divine history of Jesus and Mary, I have never come across anything more beautiful, more admirable, or more divine than the history of Joan of Arc.'"

St. Paul Book & Media Centers

ALASKA
750 West 5th Ave., Anchorage, AK 99501; 907-272-8183

CALIFORNIA
3908 Sepulveda Blvd., Culver City, CA 90230; 310-397-8676
5945 Balboa Ave., San Diego, CA 92111; 619-565-9181
46 Geary Street, San Francisco, CA 94108; 415-781-5180

FLORIDA
145 S.W. 107th Ave., Miami, FL 33174; 305-559-6715

HAWAII
1143 Bishop Street, Honolulu, HI 96813; 808-521-2731

ILLINOIS
172 North Michigan Ave., Chicago, IL 60601; 312-346-4228

LOUISIANA
4403 Veterans Memorial Blvd., Metairie, LA 70006; 504-887-7631

MASSACHUSETTS
50 St. Paul's Ave., Jamaica Plain, Boston, MA 02130; 617-522-8911
Rte. 1, 885 Providence Hwy., Dedham, MA 02026; 617-326-5385

MISSOURI
9804 Watson Rd., St. Louis, MO 63126; 314-965-3512

NEW JERSEY
561 U.S. Route 1, Wick Plaza, Edison, NJ 08817; 908-572-1200

NEW YORK
150 East 52nd Street, New York, NY 10022; 212-754-1110
78 Fort Place, Staten Island, NY 10301; 718-447-5071

OHIO
2105 Ontario Street, Cleveland, OH 44115; 216-621-9427

PENNSYLVANIA
510 Holstein Street, Bridgeport, PA 19405; 215-277-7728

SOUTH CAROLINA
243 King Street, Charleston, SC 29401; 803-577-0175

TENNESSEE
4811 Poplar Ave., Memphis, TN 38117; 901-761-0874

TEXAS
114 Main Plaza, San Antonio, TX 78205; 210-224-8101

VIRGINIA
1025 King Street, Alexandria, VA 22314; 703-549-3806

GUAM
285 Farenholt Avenue, Suite 308, Tamuning, Guam 96911; 671-646-7745

CANADA
3022 Dufferin Street, Toronto, Ontario, Canada M6B 3T5; 416-781-9131